LET THE CLOCK RUN WILD

Wit and Wisdom from Boomers and Bobbysoxers

Compiled & Edited by
Judy Warner Scher and Jewell Reinhart Coburn

English edition first published in 2014 by Generation Books

Let the Clock Run Wild: Wit and Wisdom from Boomers and Bobbysoxers
Compiled and edited by Judy Warner Scher and Jewell Reinhart Coburn
© 2014 Generation Books
The copyright for all the stories and poems in this compilation are held by their respective creators and are reproduced here with their permission.

Credits for previously published material:
Milton Teichman: *Wising up* included in short story collection, *A Teacher of the Holocaust and Other Stories*, published by Page Publishing, 2014.
Peter Mellen: *Ultimate Happiness* from *Ultimate Happiness: Chasing It, Finding It, Living It*, 2012.
Judy Scher: *A Moving Experience*, Montecito Journal, April 2010.
Cherise Wyneken: *Bent, Not Broken* published by permission, Haworth Press.
Paul Morrissey: *Let Someone Hold You* from *Let Someone Hold You: The Journey of a Hospice Priest*, Crossroads, 1994.
Leslie Westbrook: A different version of this essay, *Getting Back in the Saddle*, appeared on NextAvenue.org
Andrew Merton: *Turkey* from *Silk Road*, 2008.
Barbara Lydecker Crane: *Just Following Orders* appeared on line in *Snakeskin* (UK), April 2010.

Quotations used throughout the book are in the public domain, thus are categorized under "Fair Use."

Copyright © 2014 Judy Warner Scher
All rights reserved.

ISBN-10: 0615957145
ISBN-13: 9780615957142 (Generation Books)
Library of Congress Control Number: 2014933559
Generation Books, Santa Barbara, CA

Acknowledgments

Our heartfelt thanks go to Claire Gerus, publishing consultant, Vivian Browne and Terri Cooper for their generous encouragement and assistance throughout the life of the project.

"In my next life I want to live my life backwards. You start out dead and get that out of the way. Then you wake up in an old people's home feeling better every day. You get kicked out for being too healthy, go collect your pension, and then when you start work, you get a gold watch and a party on your first day. You work for 40 years until you're young enough to enjoy your retirement. You party, drink alcohol, and are generally promiscuous, then you are ready for high school. You then go to primary school, you become a kid, you play. You have no responsibilities, you become a baby until you are born. And then you spend your last 9 months floating in luxurious spa-like conditions with central heating and room service on tap, larger quarters every day and then Voila! You finish off as an orgasm!"

Woody Allen

Introduction

*L*et the Clock Run Wild is a collection of vibrant stories and poems, told with style and substance by writers in their 60s (Boomers), 70s and 80s (Bobbysoxers).

The treasury of stories bears witness to the infinite capacity of the human spirit at any age: Some 'put a smile on the face of life,' as in the humorous account of the tribulations and benefits of life in an assisted living facility, or when we uncover the wonder of rediscovered sex after our adult kids have finally left home. They illustrate what we do 'when life hands you a zinger;' and you emerge from an inexplicably sexless marriage, or overcome the obstacle of losing your job. They encourage us 'not to overlook the obvious' by demonstrating the still present sense of adventure as one intrepid heroine goes hang-gliding for the first time at age 70. It focuses on 'the gift of endless benefits:' how, with the passion to help others, we can actually change ourselves.

The stories bring us to that deep place of knowing, which reminds us that much is to be found accessible to the inquiring mind and the open heart.

The editors were inspired to put this volume together after working alongside seniors and listening to stories that openly expressed sensitivity, wisdom and humor. Each story in the anthology is told with a richness of human thought and emotion. Although some may feel invisible in our youth oriented culture, the narratives and poems frequently demonstrate an exhilarating sense of freedom because the writer is finally liberated from the constraints of youth and responsibility.

What we learned and now share with you is that hidden within the day-to-day stuff of life, as well as within the larger, more conflicting life events, reside gems of rarity and rich meaning. We can all too easily overlook, and continue on unaware, of what lies within our very grasp. The longer we live, certainly the more the opportunities we have to consider what life has for us in terms of revelations, insights, and life's greatest gift of all – wisdom, but always with a little bit of wit thrown in.

Those of us who are now in our sixth decade and beyond have experienced decades of life challenges and rewards: from the aftermath of World War I, the Great Depression of the 1930s, World War II, the era of post-war prosperity of the 1950s, the social revolution typified by the 60s, the technical burst forward of the 70s, with the years leading to and past the new millennium, stamped by global interaction via our personal computers.

Due to these experiences and the advances in healthcare and technology, we are no longer limited by our chronological age. So, why not just *Let YOUR Clock Run Wild?*

Table of Contents

Part 1: Putting a Smile on the Face of Life   1

Terri Cooper	*Confessions of a Martian Émigré*	3
Ed Meek	*When the Chips are Down*	11
V.H. Josenhans	*Revenge is a Dish Best Served* Old	15
Arleen Weissman	*Poem: Please Hold*	19
Diane Caldwell	*Do Not Go Gentle*	21
Sara Nuss-Galles	*Fast, Cheap and Out of Control*	27
Karen Miyashiro	*Spandex: Miracle or Madness*	33
James Ciletti	*Poem: Don't Rush Me*	37
Mike Senzamici	*Tale of a Six Legged Man*	39
David Barnhouse	*What Happened to Your Eye?*	47
Vivian Browne	*Love in the Time of Dementia*	51

Part 2: Don't Overlook The Obvious   57

Judith Geller	*It's Never Too Late for Adventure*	59
Jack Malken	*You Just Don't Listen*	63
Milton Teichman	*Wising Up*	67
Peter Mellen	*Ultimate Happiness*	79
Michael Levy	*Poem: His Milestone*	87
C.A. Fiore	*No Man is an Island*	91

Jewell R. Coburn	*Everyday Alchemy*	97
Andrew Merton	*Poem: Turkey*	107
Joe Novara	*Dying in the Pulpit*	109
Judy Warner Scher	*A Moving Experience*	113

Part 3: When Life Hands You A Zinger — 117

Nancy Katz	*Blindsided*	119
Diana Amadeo	*Blessed*	123
R. R. Hart	*Into the Unknown*	127
Rosie Loew	*Pink Slip*	133
Janet Hines	*The Last Sail*	141
Barbara Lydecker Crane	*Poem: Just Following Orders*	149
Doris Thome	*A Different Farewell*	151
Kathy Marden	*What a Shame, She Has Such a Pretty Face*	157
J. R. Reinhart	*The Yellow Bathtub*	161
Donald Shephard	*Never Surrender*	169
Annie Jacobs	*Poem: Rant*	177

Part 4: The Gift Of Endless Benefits — 179

Maril Crabtree	*A Shiny Stick of Love*	181
Elayne Clift	*A Circle of Crones*	187
Cherise Wyneken	*Bent, Not Broken*	193
Jean Gardner	*Urged to Action*	199
Paul Morrissey	*Let Someone Hold You*	213
Linda Mellen	*Poem: I Am*	219
Linda Berkery	*Touchstones of Faith*	221

Doris Thome	*A Promise to Keep*	225
Jeannette Caruth	*Poem: Life*	233

Part 5: My Body; My Mind; My Spirit; Myself — 235

R. J. Burnhart	*A Kind of Magic*	237
Leslie A. Westbrook	*Getting Back in the Saddle*	245
Susan Chan Egan	*A Well Nigh Unattainable Ideal*	251
Ronald Pies, M.D.	*Let the Small Clocks Run Wild*	261
Maureen Flannery	*Poem: Aspect of Aging*	267
Jim Van Buskirk	*Enough Space to See Myself*	269
Vidya Vonne	*One Treasure I Know*	277
Doris Thome	*Final Adventure*	281
Julian Langley	*Crash to Crash: A Longer View*	287
Ken Cohen	*Poem: Let the Clock Run Wild*	297

Appendix	298
About the Editors	300

PART 1

Putting A Smile on the Face of Life

"Age is an issue of mind over matter. If you don't mind, it doesn't matter."

Mark Twain

CONFESSIONS OF A MARTIAN ÉMIGRÉ

Terri Cooper, M.A., MFT

Here I stand in the spotlight, applause ringing in my ears, performing as a stand-up comic for the first time at the ripe old age of 68 – and loving every minute of it.

Standing up in front of people isn't new to me. (I've been a teacher for 30 years). But being funny in front of a live audience – *that* is new to me.

I've always been able to make people laugh. Bet you didn't know that Martians are naturally funny. We are though, but more about my origins later. Growing up taught me that if you can make people laugh, they are less likely to hit you. So I became a funny kid, which happily saved my skinny little backside on many occasions, both with my dysfunctional family and on the rough streets of Brooklyn, New York.

I grew up in the 50's in what is known as a culturally Jewish family – which meant we celebrated the Jewish holiday feasts but weren't observant Jews who regularly went to Temple. Did you know that there are Jews on Mars too? They don't call us wanderers for nothing. My family held a relatively truncated view of the raison d'être of the Jewish holidays – which seemed to boil down to that old Jewish adage: "They tried to kill us. We won. Let's eat." And *that* we did religiously.

We did go to temple at least once a year on the high holy days of Yom Kippur – the time when God does a life review of every Jewish person and decides if He will inscribe them in the Book of Life for a good year. It's a nervous time for all but the most secular of Jews. My mother, wanting to be certain we had the best shot for a better year than the one we just had, made sure we were pious for at least these two high holy days. Part of the required ritual during Yom Kippur was to pray and fast for one full day from sundown to sundown. We hoped that the sound of our stomachs grumbling from hunger would convince God of our holiness and encourage him to grant us peace and prosperity. So far, like Santa Claus had done, God had skipped our house, but I guess hope springs eternal.

At the end of the 24 hours of fasting and prayer, it is customary to have a light dinner of chicken soup and let your stomach get used to eating again. This, however, was not the custom in my house. My wonderful, wacky mother, always playing to the crowd (imagined or otherwise) fed our ravenous family our favorite food: Italian lasagna, served with a chaser of Pepto Bismol for the inevitable indigestion that came from fasting and then feasting.

While other religious beliefs and rituals weren't practiced in my home, what was honored and what I had always been taught to accept and recognize were my intuitive gifts. Growing up, my earliest memories were of the family stories that revolved around my grandmother and great grandmother being the soothsayers in their native Romanian villages.

While I was aware of my family's history of intuitive acumen, it was not the only influence on my eventual development as a Transpersonal Psychotherapist and all around funny lady. My life was very much informed by my Mom's own unique way of looking at life and dealing with both a lousy marriage and a depressed son. She is what made it all bearable for me growing up. In fact, believe it or not, a number of the episodes portrayed in the 1950's comedy "The Honeymooners" were taken directly from life with my father. You see, my mother's brother, Coleman Jacoby, wrote many of the episodes of that historic comedy. He got a lot of his story lines from my mother who would tell him about her crazy life with my father. When I tell people who remember this show that my father was the template for the Jackie Gleason character "Ralph Kramden," they find this fascinating. But living it wasn't fascinating at all. Remember the famous line Ralph would always use when he was upset with his wife, Alice? He would glare at her, raise his fist and say "To the moon Alice, straight to the moon." If you recall that, you'll probably also remember that every episode would end with Ralph taking Alice into his arms and telling her, "Baby, you're the greatest!" Well that ending didn't happen in my house. The endings at my house, more often than not, were anything but a honeymoon.

To keep our life from being relentlessly grim, my amazing mother could take the darkest day and find a way to brighten it with her irrepressible joy of living and her wacky sense of humor. So while my dad was the model for the bombastic and easily provoked Ralph Kramden, my mother was definitely no "Alice." Long suffering, yes, but with a wonderful sense of humor and the ability to make lemonade out of lemons like no one I've ever met before or since. I guess she inherited the family comedy gene because life with my mother and my brother, who would occasionally enter into cahoots with her, was never grim and definitely never dull.

My mother truly identified with Lucille Ball's character Lucy Ricardo in "I Love Lucy." Lucy was forever getting into wacky situations that made for wildly funny episodes on the Lucy Show. Like her successful writer brother, my Mom had a wild imagination, which she couldn't share with my father. But it certainly got shared with me.

One Saturday morning, when I was about 6 years old, my mom was letting me style her hair. As I moved her hair this way and that, I noticed two small scars right at the top of her head.

"Mom," I said lightly touching the scars, "Where did you get these?"

My mother got this "Lucy" look in her eye and bending down to whisper in a conspiratorial tone said, "Well, I guess you're old enough to know the truth Terri, we're not really from Earth. We're from Mars. The scars you see are where my antenna was removed when we landed here."

Well, this was certainly not the answer I expected to hear at 9:00 in the morning, right after my bowl of Wheaties. "So Mom," I said gingerly feeling the top of my head, "Where are my antennas?"

Mom smiled and replied "Oh, honey, we had your antennae removed at birth by a very skilled Martian surgeon and, well, you were so young, the scars are just too small to see."

I believed her, mind boggling though this news was. Why? Because moms don't lie, right, especially when they're telling you secrets? Eventually I found out that her scars had come from burns she received while having a permanent wave.

But this was the beginning of the running gag she and my brother, who occasionally came out of his depressive funk, played on me about our being Martian Émigrés with very special powers.

Another interesting fact I discovered about Martians is that they can perform surgeries. I found this out one evening when I was about 7. Mom came home later than expected, and I was upset because I was hungry and I wanted my dinner. Mom got that Lucy twinkle in her eye again and breathlessly explained why she was late.

"I had to perform an emergency appendectomy on Sylvia Diamond. It was just too late to call the doctor, and so I had to perform the surgery on her kitchen table with a carving knife. The good news is that she's all sewed up now and feeling much better, and that's why I'm late, honey."

I was awestruck at the thought of my mother carving up our upstairs neighbor. I pictured fat little Mrs. Diamond, like one of her plump Friday night stewed chickens, lying naked on her kitchen table with her family gathered around, slurping their chicken soup, as they watched my mother remove her appendix – whatever that was. I knew my Mom cooked a mean lasagna but who knew she was also a surgeon? I concluded this must be another Martian trait because I didn't know any other mothers who performed surgeries on dinner tables. I figured Mrs. Diamond must have healed pretty quickly because a bit later, as my family sat eating our dinner, we heard Mrs. Diamond yelling her favorite threat at her youngest son, as she chased him around the kitchen table with a knife in her hand, "If you don't behave, Stanley, I'm going to cut your little shmecky off with my knife."

Honest to God, that's what she used to threaten him with all the time. Apparently she never carried out her threat, thank God, because Stanley grew up to marry and have 3 kids. But then again who knows, maybe she did and called on my mother to perform a secret re-attachment shmeckyectomy on Stanley.

Speaking of strange surgeries – one day when I was about 8, I asked my brother about this clay head he had sculpted and kept on the kitchen shelf. "Art," I said, "why do you keep that dumb clay head in the closet?"

He stared directly into my eyes and in a very serious voice informed me, "This is your other head, Kiddo. All Martian girls get fitted for their second heads when they turn 18 – so that's why I'm saving it."

I narrowed my eyes and stared at him for a long time, but he just looked so damn sincere. Martians, apparently, are also very good liars. "Yeah, right," I laughed nervously.

For years after that, as I blew out my birthday candles, my brother would wistfully remark, "Only 8 more years to go until you get your second head." On through the years, "Only 7 more years... only six more years..." Never mind that no one else in the family had two heads, my brother assured me that when the time came, I would be fitted for my second head – like it or not. Admittedly I was a bit gullible when it came to my family's stories but even *I* knew that this was crazy. Still, when someone tells you the same thing year after year, it does give one pause.

When I turned 18, as I was blowing out the candles on my birthday cake, I glanced up to see my brother smiling at me while pointing at my neck and then at the 18 candles on my birthday cake. What my dear brother didn't know was that morning while he slept, I had taken the damned clay head and tossed it in the garbage can outside our house. I figured better safe than sorry. Who knew what he would do to prove his running gag true. Smiling back at him I pointed to the empty top shelf of the closet and returned his gesture with a middle finger salute.

Through the years I've made many friends with my ability to make people laugh and lighten up when things get too heavy. And, like my mother, I am often able to defuse potential disasters with a well-timed humorous comment.

A few years ago I was officiating a wedding at an upscale, private Christian school in the tony area of Montecito, located just south of Santa Barbara, California. The ceremony was being held in an elegant chapel of the school. As I watched from the side of the stage, the room filled with the wealthy and sedate family and friends of the young couple. As I looked at them I felt compelled to perform a flawless ceremony so as not to ruffle one fancy feather in that room. Several minutes passed and we were notified that the bride was standing outside the chapel door and that the processional consisting of myself, the groom and his groomsmen, were to walk onto the stage so that the ceremony could begin. There was only one problem – the groom's alcoholic brother, who was his 'best man,' was nowhere to be found. As time passed, I heard the crowd growing restless, and I stopped feeling like the confident, accomplished Wedding Officiant I knew I was, and I became that skinny little Jewish kid from Brooklyn about to face a room full of uptight fancy Gentiles. As I stood there, my anxiety growing by the minute, I muttered to myself "Oh, shit." When I heard the collective gasp from the guests seated in the chapel, I realized, in horror, that my lapel microphone was 'live' and that they had just heard what the Wedding Officiant said.

Luckily, the old survival technique kicked in and I calmly said out loud, "Sorry, folks, I meant to say "Holy Shit." The ripple of laughter that followed allowed me to exhale with a sigh of relief. The best man was eventually found and the wedding proceeded smoothly with everyone in good spirits, thanks to the gift of quick wit that my funny Momma had left me.

My wonderful mother taught me an invaluable lesson that has stood me in good stead all my life: Find a way to make the best of the cards that are dealt you. She taught me that even though you may cry often, laughter is always possible – just around the corner.

As my debut performance ended to rousing applause and laughter I knew, as I took my bow, that mom would be proud of me and that she was no doubt applauding joyously somewhere in heaven – or even – somewhere on Mars.

Terri Cooper, M.A.MFT resides in Santa Barbara, CA having moved there from Los Angeles after the Northridge earthquake. For 30 years Terri has been a psychotherapist, stand-up comedienne, a psychology and transpersonal educator at Santa Barbara City College and a professional Intuitive and Medium. This is Terri's first published story.

WHEN THE CHIPS ARE DOWN

Ed Meek

By sixty you are who you are. This means that there is no more lying. I don't mean lying to others, but lying to yourself. What's the point to it anymore – trying to be what you aren't? Bill Clinton knows that he's a rake. He's trying to make up for it by helping others, especially Hillary.

One of the things I've been thinking about is to stop fooling around with my health, trying to convince myself I'm still in great shape. It's time to begin to live a healthier life. To start cutting down on the booze. You can't drink anymore anyway. More than three drinks and you can't sleep. You can't drink and drive. If you do you may forget to turn on your lights. Since you can't see as well at night, you drive too slowly or you take the exit too fast and, let me tell you something, there is nothing more embarrassing than getting pulled over for drinking and driving at this stage of life. I got pulled over last year when I had four beers (watching the NCAA play-offs with a friend at a local bar). I wasn't drunk but the cop (who couldn't have been more than twelve years old) wouldn't believe me. He had my car towed. It was only after I took a Breathalyzer test at the station that they let me go. I slunk home and the next morning paid eighty bucks to retrieve my car.

You could step up the exercise too. You see a lot of people over sixty these days jogging and playing tennis and going to the gym. I try to run three or four times a week. In fact I ran a marathon last spring but I had to walk the last six miles. It took me four and a half hours. If I were running to warn the Athenians, the city would be under siege by the time I got there. I also lift weights for twenty minutes two or three days a week. I try to do this around five in the afternoon but if I am tired or don't feel like it, I skip it and have a beer instead.

A few years ago on a whim I decided to try snowboarding under the impression that it would be easier on my knees than skiing. It turns out that snowboarding is easier on the knees, but a minor drawback is you fall all the time. Where it's okay to fall when you are ten, twenty, even thirty, a fall at sixty can result in nagging injuries. I know! I sprained my wrist on New Year's Day and it was two months before I could lift weights again. And although snowboarding is easier on the knees, I had to be taken down the mountain on a rescue sled last winter when my back went out.

Another problem is not with snowboarding itself but with what it brings to light and that is – fear. Don't tell anyone about this because it is a secret among guys, but fear begins to sneak up on you in your forties and by the time you're sixty, it has taken up residence in your house. I bought a nice twenty-eight foot fiberglass ladder so I could reach the eaves. I used to work as a painter in the summers when I was in college so I thought I knew what I was doing but now, whenever I climb up on that ladder, I have to psych myself up. I get nervous up there. I can see the headlines: Man About to be Blown Off Ladder Rescued by Local Fire Department. (How embarrassing.)

The other problem with snowboarding is that snowboarders do jumps. The little jumps, one or two feet high are fine but my son, who is twenty, likes to do the big jumps, the ten and fifteen footers, which are giant white cliffs of snow created by the deranged men who groom the slopes at night. In my mind's eye I can make these jumps. After all, I was a gymnast in high school. But right there is the problem. My mind plays tricks on me – letting me remember my glory days when I was fit and agile. But when I try to act on those memories, my body lets me know real fast who is boss. Don't tell anyone but I often make myself fall down on purpose while approaching take-off. How else is an old guy to slow down before landing?

I've learned too it's better I fall than my son. If anything happens to him, I may start weeping. That's another thing, I've become very emotional, very sensitive. I often find myself choking up watching television shows or movies or reading novels. Newspaper stories can also make me lose it. Old photos? Forget it. In short, I've become sentimental. Of course, this is better than being the callous, devil-may-care fool I was in my twenties.

Perhaps the Russians have the right idea. In Chekhov's plays, a man of sixty is in his prime—at the top of his career—ready to settle down and marry. I've read personals that say: 'Sixty and fabulous.' And I have to admit some older women do look great. There's Cher Surgery, Goldie-still-cute-Hawn, Susan-still-sexy-Sarandon.

Bill Nye was right when he claimed, "Science rules." Maybe science will rescue us. That could be good news for us in terms of longevity, replacement parts, memory enhancement and cures for many of the diseases that plague us seniors. We'll leave the next generation to deal with implanting computer chips, genetic manipulation, cyborgs and clone clans. But in another thirty years, when my son will be dealing with these changes, I won't have anything to say about it. I'll be enjoying the big sleep.

Okay, so I'm being disingenuous. There are some things about being sixty that make it much better than I thought it would be. I am, after all, able to run (I ran a 1:48 half marathon last fall); I do lift weights, snowboard, and enjoy sex. I also know what's good in wine, food, cigars, books, magazines and movies. And in the mornings I seem to be able to see even more clearly the way the light strikes the trees, illuminates the grass, infiltrates the water. And I don't mind hearing the song sparrow outside my window at five a.m. because I'm already awake anyway. The sunsets seem to be getting better too.

So, I guess what I'm trying to say is, you could call turning sixty a mixed bag, which is a lot better than being an old bag.

Ed Meek has been published in the *Paris Review, The Sun, The North American Review, The Boston Globe*. His latest book of poems is *What We Love*.

REVENGE IS A DISH BEST SERVED *OLD*

V.H. Josenhans

It isn't that I mind getting old. Or, at least, older than I used to be. (*Absolutes, are so, well, absolute, don't you think?*) It is not even that I resent others their youth. It is just that I have come to realize that with age comes freedom. And, as has always been true: with freedom has come responsibility.

So, it is my responsibility, I have decided, to...well, to demonstrate to our children how we have lived long enough to exact retribution. Or, to take the higher road: not to get mad – but to get even.

So, it is with great satisfaction that I inform my children, (*as often as I am able*), that I now take more drugs than they ever did. And, I get them for free. And legally. (*Mostly!*)

And, what perverse pleasure there is, as a guest in their homes, in coming back at 3 a.m., after a night out with an old friend (or flame) to still-awake children, looking tight-lipped at their watches with a frustrated, (*and disapproving?*) look on their faces. The next morning they inquire as to why I hadn't called, just to let them know I was safe and that I would be late.

Of course, they do not touch on sex, because they cannot imagine that we might. But, if they can conceive of it, they warn us to be careful, because it is a different world out there now. (*Have they never heard of the '60s?*)

As to their looks of concern in your rear view mirror as you hot rod it down the road in your new two-seater red convertible? Priceless!

And what inner smiles when they beg you to turn off the radio in your car on the few occasions that they get up the courage to drive with you? That is, when they are not returning the favor of the driving lessons that you gave them, lo, those many years ago.

So, how about being required to check in with *them* at the end of every day when you have decided to take a cross-country driving trip – on your own – which they have reluctantly agreed to – or rather realized their powerlessness in stopping? Otherwise, they will stay sleepless with worry, they say. (*Sound familiar?*)

And, after paying hundreds of thousands for their finicky food choices, their labeled clothing and private schooling, it is finally costing them to support *you* via their contributions to Social Security and Medicare. Contributions about which they are complaining loudly. Or, threatening to vote Republican!

What delight to see their faces as you pour as much salt and sugar on your food as you want. Personally, I have watched my diet and eaten healthily practically all of my life. Now, since simple arithmetic and insurance mortality tables have assured that no matter what we do, we cannot add that many more years to our lives – why not live it out to the fullest, and eat – and do – all those things that we have avoided for so long? On those fewer and fewer occasions when I still hesitate, I revert to my son's late teen logic that, since he had twelve years on everyone else by having eaten healthily as a child, he could eat all the junk food he craved. Well, me too.

And let's not forget the opportunity to finally embarrass *them* as they introduce us to their friends: We can wear too much make-up, and grubby clothing – and claim it is because we don't see so well in the mirror. Our hair can be rinsed too pink, or too blue, or, dyed too black (*at what age does 'goth' turn into 'old witch'?*) And our outfit can be too loose (*have they never seen Annie Hall?*) or – ('*OMG*') - too tight! If we sneeze, or, even better, select the most expensive steak on the menu (their treat,) they will just be praying that our teeth don't fall out.

And, what about our remorselessly accumulated (*for them, of course*) treasures, priceless and irreplaceable – if a little retro – that we will leave for them to clean up and sort through when we are gone. Though, perhaps we will be able to peer, devilishly, over their shoulders and haunt them as they guiltily discard most of it.

But, in the end, our greatest act of retribution might just be one that was not entirely intentional: In this day of fast thought, short attention spans and shrinking resources, but 'plenty' of sugar substitutes; low-fat everything; faster growing – and eaten – food, we are bequeathing our children potentially shorter life spans, epidemic rates of diabetes and asthma, and an ever increasing incidence of auto-immune diseases and Alzheimer's. As well as a planet that appears to be warming at an alarming rate.

(To make up for this, I have decided to forego payback for 4 times a day spoon feedings... and for years of changing their diapers!)

But, for now – well, we will still be able to torment them by the way we just keep showing up......

After all, you know what they say: *"Living well [and long] is the best revenge.*

V.H. Josenhans is an English expat now living in California. She is a writer and the mother of two adult American children.

PLEASE HOLD

Arleen Weisman

Thank you for calling; our menu has changed.
If you know your extension, enter it now.
    G-O-D
That line is busy. Please hold.
Your call will be answered in the order it was received,
Or, press the pound key for more options.

Due to the large amount of callers,
Your approximate wait time is – a lifetime.
If this is urgent, hang up and call again.

Thank you for calling. Our menu has changed.
If you know your extension, enter it now.
    S-A-T-A-N
Press 1 for the devil, 2 for the evil one, 3 for Lucifer.

Devil here. How may I tempt you?
    Please get me through to extension G-O-D.
No problem. God is right here, there and everywhere.
    Thank you evil one.

Hello Almighty, just a quick question:
Why must I go through all hell to reach you?

I have been known to have little patience, yet I can sit all day on the beach listening to the waves waiting patiently for the sunset. In my eighth decade I discovered another outlet for my emotions – writing poetry. My very first poem, *Move On,* was published in 2011 entitled *Songs from the Heart.*

DO NOT GO GENTLE

Diane Caldwell

Psych 101. The exam question read: *A fifty-five-year-old women is dressed in a short-skirt, high-top trainers, and a T-shirt with the name of an alternative group across its front. This is an example of* _____ (Fill in the blank).

Clearly the answer the professor was looking for was: "Denial." I wrote my response, and then below the question I wrote: I know the answer you deem correct is "Denial." However, I ask you, at what age is it "normal" and "healthy" for a woman to stop being contemporary and start wearing formless, flowered muu muus around the house, eating bons bons and watching daytime soap operas?

The teacher called me over after she had read the exams and actually thanked me for my input.

"You have a valid point," she said, "I've removed the question from the quiz. It's frightening," she confided in me, "to realize how much we're all effected by certain societal norms."

Because, after all, what is age? What does a chronological number mean in this day of modern medicine, sanitation, vaccinations, antibiotics, vitamin pills and health tonics?

When I was a child my widowed grandmother used to sit in the same over-stuffed armchair every day, the bottom cushion indented by the shape of her posterior. She watched the same soap operas every day from eleven to one. Then she turned off the TV and sat drumming her fingers on the arm of the chair. At times, when she became lost in her own private universe of loneliness, forgetting that I sat silently reading in the next room, she would momentarily stop her finger drumming, raise her head and call out to her dead husband: "David, I wish I was in the grave with you!"

By the age of twelve I had decided to die by the time I was twenty-five. I was not only going to "burn my candle at both ends," I was firmly dedicated to cutting my candle in half, and burning all four ends. No one was going to find me sitting in an over-stuffed armchair drumming my fingers and calling out to a deceased partner in a cold grave.

It's funny how life plays out. I'm now sixty-four. Life certainly didn't turn out the way I'd planned. I'm still alive, and far, far from drumming my fingers, waiting for death to release me from my pain.

At sixty-four, I'm still a wild woman out dancing at least twice a week, smiling and greeting strangers in the street, budget-traveling solo through India, living in Istanbul, surrounded by a family of friends half my age.

The beauty of being sixty-four is that I just don't care what people think anymore. I've learned that no matter what I do in life, some people will think it's great, while others will condemn you. I figure, I might as well just make myself happy, as long as it doesn't hurt anyone else.

While recently budget-traveling through India, I boarded a state bus. As there's nowhere to stash luggage on these public buses, I hauled my backpack up and pushed it behind the driver's seat, then I lurched my way through the mass of people to a bench toward the middle where three very thin people shared the seat. Knowing that on Indian State buses this seat, designed for three, is usually shared by four people, I made my way over to it. Before sitting down, I attempted to push my small day pack onto the high shelf against the window. The stretch proved difficult because of the small space between the ceiling and the narrow shelf. I leaned over my fellow seat mates, and pushed and strained. Unable to complete my mission, holding my pack, I took a breath and prepared to try again. Then I noticed everyone in the bus watching this spectacle as if it were a reality TV program. Invigorated by my audience, I inhaled, lifted my pack, and with my full power shoved it onto the shelf.

Having successfully achieved my goal, I looked around at all the dark-eyed faces staring at me. Playing to my audience, I assumed several body builder poses, flexing my biceps above and below my head, then took a deep bow to the front, middle, and back of the bus.

With that, everyone burst into laughter and in seconds I was flooded by questions from my fellow passengers. We all engaged in conversation and at the first stop, one bench-mate bought me masala cashews, another mango juice. Just like that, I had made a bus load of new friends.

And so I try to live my life.

Yesterday, a young, Turkish musician friend invited me to join him and a group of musicians and jugglers that had been hired to perform at the annual Bakirkoy Mental Hospital Party. The Bakirkoy Psychiatric Hospital is Turkey's biggest and most famous psychiatric facility.

How could I pass up such an opportunity?

I boarded the van sent by the hospital along with twenty young Turks, their instruments and amps, hula hoops, juggling pins, and red clown noses.

Along the highway, people in cars stared into the van wondering, logically, if it was full of crazy people. And I'm sure it looked like it was.

We arrived in a big garden filled with patients and visitors, nurses and custodians, orderlies and other staff. My friends took the stage and the music started.

At first people were shy to get up and dance. But I leapt to my feet and started shimmying and shaking and encouraged others to join me. Soon the area in front of the stage was filled. Patients, nurses, children, elderly - all dancing together. I stood opposite one patient after another engaging them in joyful dance. Their faces filled with happiness and open smiles, tears filling my eyes with the beauty of it.

Every day is a new opportunity to share and rejoice with fellow human beings. Every day brings new faces, new eyes, new opinions and ideas to learn from and interface with.

I don't tell other people how to live, we're all different. But I've granted myself the freedom to live. To live fully. To take risks. To challenge myself daily. I laugh at my mistakes, try constantly to keep learning, and I'm kind and loving to myself.

After all, what's the alternative?

Eleven years ago, stifling sobs, Diane Caldwell boarded a plane to Greece. She hasn't lived in the US since. She's crossed a corner of the Sahara on a camel named Bob Marley, eaten ant-egg soup with betel-nut-chewing Thai women, and shouted "Govinda!" with Hindu pilgrims. She currently lives in Istanbul where she dances with Gypsies and writes about her experiences. You can follow her on her blog: http://dianewanderer.blogspot.co

FAST, CHEAP AND OUT OF CONTROL

A Love Story

Sara Nuss-Galles

"Do you guys do anything different now?" Arden asked during a visit home recently. We were in the middle of one of those pleasurable daughter-mother conversations that we began having after she moved to London quite a few years ago.

"Different like what?" I asked slyly. Could my adult daughter be asking what I thought she was asking?

"You know," Arden said. "Since Josh and I moved out of the house and there's no one around, do you and Dad do anything ... you know, different."

"Oh," I said, a wave of unmaternal lasciviousness washing over me. "Like are we barbecuing in the nude or making it on the kitchen counter or under the glass coffee table in the den? Is that the kind of different you mean?"

"Mom, TMI, give me a break," she laughed. "It's just a general kind of question, Mom. I don't want details, or pictures, or anything, really," she teased, averting her face from the age-old horror of imagining parents and sex in any combination.

"Well, we do have two impressionable felines at home, you know, so we try to be good role-models. Let me think," I said. I got up from the table to pour more coffee into my mug. I was actually stalling for time.

I wasn't sure what kind of answer to give her. Of course honesty is nice. But just as there are some things I prefer not to know about my kids' lives now as adults, or during their misspent youths either, I believe that there are things they might not want to know about their parents. And I'm sure that is especially true in the romance arena.

Naturally my thoughts went to the conjugal trysts that began a few years after Joshua was born and became a highlight of our marriage. "Fast, cheap and out of control," was how Alex characterized our deliciously illicit liaisons. To which I always added, "Only if we're lucky."

By this time we were safely married with a conjugal bed at our disposal, as well as all-the-rage orange shag carpeting and gold-speckled Formica counter tops, so teasing about our wicked behavior was fun. But we soon learned that those backdrops weren't always where our thrills lay.

The inspiration for our "fast, cheap and out of control" trysts sprang from the passionate months after we fell so desperately in love. Since we both lived with our families there was no place to be alone. In the mid 1960's, living together before marriage was not an option. My parents would have had apoplexy, their nosy friends would have had a field day, and even among our own friends, I might have been branded with a capital S for slut. The swinging part of the 1960's was yet to begin.

"Why buy the cow if you can get the milk for free," girls like me were warned from the day we graduated from cloth diapers to "big-girl underpants." In other words, nice girls were raised to keep their pants on until they were safely married. Discretion ruled before the free-living flower children changed the rules a short time later. You either tried the goods discretely or not at all. Unfortunately, discretion was neither my nor Albert's strong point.

In Chicago, the best lovers' lanes overlook Lake Michigan. No matter the season, the beachside parking lots were crowded with hormonally charged youth watching what were slyly referred to as the submarine races – otherwise known as necking. Albert and I joined them and, it wasn't long before physics took over and the frigid outdoor temperature collided with the heat within. Our lust was consummated in the back of a 1963 Mercury Marquis. Fortunately, Albert's meticulous parents had the foresight to scotch-guard the deep-burgundy interior fabric. The seat was narrower than a single bed and the power windows operated on a hair trigger, but we hardly noticed.

To borrow a phrase from rock and roller Meatloaf, we learned about love by the glow of the dashboard light, as did many of our generation. Mostly, our background was top 40 music played by disc jockeys like Wolfman Jack. However, in the wee hours we thrilled to the Night Bird, a jazz aficionado whose velvet-tones made Clorets Breath Mints sound like Love Potion #9.

After Albert and I married, the winter escapades and reeking ashtrays were abandoned and we luxuriated in a real bed in our own little apartment. Then the kids came and our bed became as much family territory as the kitchen table. Once they starting walking, Josh and later Arden joined us anytime they woke during the night. They also piled on top of us every morning. Yet again we had no place to be alone.

Eventually, this young wife and mother began fantasizing about our stolen hours in the Marquis. I conveniently forgot all the fears I'd experienced as patrol cars circled the lots bent on keeping the youth of America chaste. If a head or two wasn't visible the cops delighted in announcing themselves with a blinding spotlight. It could be embarrassing.

But, necessity *is* the mother of invention. I recall that it began during a particularly promising spring. Buds thickened trees and branches, forsythia and willows grew fuzzy with blossoms, and, Albert and I hadn't had a peaceful night in months. The first time we reverted to our old trick we hired a babysitter and announced that we were going to a movie and would be home in about three hours.

We drove to the lake and parked our four-door sedan between two station wagons – other parents trying to get some Mick Jagger-style satisfaction? Probably not. But whoever our neighbors were, we felt totally gleeful. At least we knew we were guaranteed to get lucky.

Wolfman Jack and the Nightbird were history, but we popped in a Cruisin' Classics tape we'd bought at a local gas station for $2.99 with a fill-up. We had also laid in our comforts: a pillow, a towel, a soft blanket (our Volvo had vinyl seats *and* they were even smaller than the old Marquis), and for after, a nice snack, as befitting a properly married couple. Suffice it to say, it was heaven. And, yes, Albert and I agreed, "It was fast, cheap and out of control."

That was the beginning of an occasional date that went on for many years. When the kids began borrowing the car they occasionally cramped our plans, but the enforced spontaneity made up for it. And, interestingly enough, even after they moved out we continued meeting that way from time to time. Admittedly, our acrobatics over the years became adapted to rotator-cuff limitations, cramped calves, meniscal knee-tears, or whatever aches we're nursing at the time. But, our dates remain deliciously dirty.

Back in the kitchen I look over at my dear daughter Arden. It appears that she waited so long for my answer that she immersed herself in reading the horoscope column in the local newspaper. Then I swish my room temperature coffee around in my cup as if I'm attempting to read tea leaves. I'd gotten a bit lost in my reveries.

"Do we do anything different now that we're alone, you wanted to know." My daughter turns her sweet, open face to me and I decide that honesty is, after all, the best policy. "No, things haven't changed all that much. You know, dear, like it said, while love's flames become a bit tempered with time, for your Dad and me, our coals, we find, are still hot."

Sara Nuss-Galles has published her personal essays and humor widely, including *The New York Times*, *The Los Angeles Times* and *Lilith*. Her work was featured in *Nice Jewish Girls, When Memory Speaks, The Holocaust in Art* and other anthologies. She and her husband and adored felines live in Southern California.

"My grandmother started walking five miles a day when she was sixty. She's ninety-seven now, and we don't know where the heck she is."
                                                                              Ellen DeGeneres

SPANDEX: MADNESS OR MIRACLE

Karen Miyashiro

I knew I was losing my figure; that is, I knew I was getting squishy. And since it was part of aging, there were a limited number of solutions for this, the sensible ones being working out and plastic surgery. I'm short on energy and money, so I chose Option Number Three – denial.

If you stop tucking in your shirts, you don't have to acknowledge that your waist is gone. Keep your clothes on; never acknowledge your amount of skin and flab. If the only mirrors in your house are the bathroom type above the counter, you never even have to *see* anything below your chest. The only time I had to confront my expanded size was at the hairdresser's, where the mirror showed the whole chair and, there they were, my thighs oozing over the sides.

Anyway, my dearest friend was getting married in July, and in May she asked me to be her matron of honor, in fact her only attendant, at this her second wedding. I said yes without even thinking. Well, my friend knew I didn't have much in the way of disposable income, so she decided to buy everything for me: dress, shoes, jewelry, and a couple of other things. She was so happy to do it.

Of course, it never occurred to me that I wouldn't be able to actually see the dress she chose until she brought it to me. She had chosen pale yellow, a color that makes me look jaundiced. She was so proud when she and her daughter brought me actually two dresses to choose from – both the color of butter. No, I take that back – both the color of margarine. Is this a choice?

We do have one full length mirror in the house, tucked behind the door in what was my daughter's room, and since there were going to be pictures and other people around at this occasion, I had to see what *all* of me was going to look like. The first dress I tried was a size 8. I'm not petite anymore, but this dress looked like a vat of butter-cream frosting exploded on me. There was yellow satin *everywhere*. The bodice was huge and baggy. I looked like the Prom Queen from Hell. I knew I had to choose the second one, after all it looked okay on the hanger. It was strapless and simple, and it had a satin band at the top with a few sequins on it. And, it did fit me, more or less.

This dress was actually meant for a younger, firmer, slimmer woman – someone who rode in convertibles and drank pink champagne. Right away I saw I'd have to stand up painfully straight; thank goodness there were plastic stays in the sides to remind me not to slouch. Or breathe. When I saw myself, it was a shock; I'd been covering myself up for so long, I didn't realize just exactly how much flesh I'd grown.

OK, maybe it's not only about more flesh – it's just that there is no elasticity anymore. That happens after a few decades, you know. I knew I'd have to buy a cincher for the waistline.

So I went to Macy's and found the Intimate Apparel section called the *Shape Shop*. Sounded promising, I thought. Well, there was something for everyone of every size and shape. The garments were even labeled by their compression levels, from light shaping to things that looked like tourniquets. I started with light, but quickly advanced to tourniquets.

My first big shock was that I really had to start with Large. And even those I had trouble getting into. I wanted to commit hara kiri until I figured out that if I could actually get one of these babies on without squirming and pushing and contorting myself, I wouldn't need one anyway, even if the object was to compress 125 pounds of Jello into a space meant for 100.

Oh, and forget about Jello, these three-way mirrors now had me looking like a sausage that had exploded on each end. I had to push and move my bulk around, and stuff as much as possible back in. At one point, I actually produced pleats. Thank God, the dress would cover them up. I paid my $46 and took my tourniquet home. By this time my right eye was twitching.

I had tried on my dress to model it for my friend. She was very quiet. Then she said, "Well, you can get one of those spray tans." Guess she figured darker shapes look smaller.

So the day before the wedding, we went to a tanning parlor where there are three kinds of Spray Tan: the one you do yourself, the one a machine does, and the one we had. I felt like a car on a conveyer belt in those old Earl Scheib commercials. First, a woman in a mask uses a loud compressor to paint you on only the parts you have chosen, then you have to stand in front of fans and finally you have to wait 24 hours to take a shower, lest your custom finish rub off.

Ever since my friend had honored me with her request to be part of her wedding, I'd been dieting. I walked for 25 minutes each morning. With this routine, plus my tourniquet, I was almost *sure* the dress was going to work. But to my horror, I had actually grown *more* flesh in the interim. I was bulging over the top of the dress, and my bare arms were competing with the jowls on my face. I should've gone with the full body paint job, but it was too late now. No matter how I tried to "arrange" myself, there was just nowhere to put all this extra mushy, sallow stuff.

The wedding went beautifully. The bride was a vision of Heaven. Only two people fainted from the heat. The groom kept refilling my wine glass. And in no time, I kicked off my tight shoes and tried to distract people from looking at my figure by talking loudly and laughing a lot.

I'm going to another wedding in August.

I'm going to wear an Indian tunic with flowy pants.

K. Miyashiro is a middle-aged (over 60) single mother who currently lives in Santa Barbara, CA. She is retired and enjoys writing about her experiences.

DON'T RUSH ME

James Ciletti

Don't rush me, Pal. Summer's in the fast lane
and frost'll nip the tomatoes. Winter will
blow shivering cold, will ice my streets soon enough, – so

So don't rush me. Skin dries and wrinkles fast enough,
and my ears already call for hearing aids; did I mention
teeth, digestion, knees wobbling, low back pain?

So don't rush — chill. Now, I'll lie down under the sprinkler,
feel the thousand drops tingle my face, eat cake for breakfast,
drink some sunlight then give sunlit kisses to Mary.

I'll eat ripe tomatoes with salt, have a third cup of coffee,
dunk chocolate in it. Chill, it's still summer and
at age 120, I will dance the night before I die.

James Ciletti, 2010-2012 Pikes Peak Poet Laureate, with his wife Mary, have Hooked on Books bookstore in Colorado Springs. Jim's poems have won awards and *Sunfire*, is his latest collection of poetry. "I love all things Italian, cooking and making home-made wine." Jim's blog is http://plumlover.wordpress.com

"Be careful about reading health books. You many die of a misprint."
Mark Twain

TALE OF A SIX LEGGED MAN

Mike Senzamici

I am an amputee. It's my right leg. It's commonly known as BKA which stands for "below knee amputation." It's much better than above the knee, but there I go looking at the bright side of things. With an "above knee amputation" not only do you lose your leg, foot and ankle but also your knee. I only lost my leg, foot and ankle. Again it's the bright side.

For the last 60 years, one of my long term goals has been to keep as much of me as possible: mind body and spirit, and live forever. So far so good! I must confess however, this is not my first amputation, I've had others. When I was about a week old I was circumcised. I was brand new, sparkly clean, unused if you will, and all of a sudden snip, snip and…well you get the idea. I've also had some teeth pulled along the way. I'm not sure if haircuts and fingernail clippings count as amputations however it makes me feel better when I think everyone is an amputee in some way, and it makes me feel less odd. Again, I'm looking at the bright side.

Haircuts, fingernail clippings, circumcisions and tooth extractions aside, this is how my latest amputation happened. I was a bus driver making a daily run between Santa Barbara and

Los Angeles. I was at work one day trying to unload passengers at the airport. This entails a lot of running around and trying to serve everyone at one time. It's impossible, but a noble effort, to keep everyone happy in a stressful situation. I was done with this load of passengers and ran up a short set of stairs, hitting the second one wrong and twisting my foot and ankle. It blew up like a hot air balloon over Albuquerque in October. It was toward the end of my day and, looking at the bright side, I'd thought I'd be better by the next morning. I wasn't. It took about a week of pain and not being able to walk until I started feeling better.

I thought it was healed when about two months later it blew up again for no reason. Actually there was a reason. It never healed and I was trying to see through the pain and "self-repair." As a result I went to the doctor to be checked out and he explained that the ligaments on the outside of my right foot were damaged and as hard as I could try there wouldn't be any "self-repair" anytime soon. An outpatient surgery would be necessary. Ugh! Not one but two surgeries. Double-Ugh! I went through the first surgery to repair the ligaments and it went so well I was actually looking forward to the second operation.

The second surgery was to correct the damage to the bone that the ligament damage had done. I went into this operation looking forward to the day I could walk normally again and chuck my crutches.

During the healing process I noticed a small amount of dripping behind my heel. That was where the doctor had put in the screw to hold the whole heel together. I went back to the doctor and he confirmed it was infected. He instructed me to put on some ointment he wrote a prescription for, and a band aid, and to see him in a week. He announced that, "This is a nightmare." I thought he was being overly sympathetic to my situation; it sounded almost like an apology.

After weeks and weeks of seeing him for three minutes and hearing "this is a nightmare," he finally sent me to an infectious disease specialist.

By this time the infection was showing through the bottom of my foot as well. The new I.D. doctor got serious and recommended I have hyperbaric treatments. For those not familiar with this thrill ride, it consists of being locked in a coffin...I mean a chamber, air tight, sealed, like on a gurney where they put dead bodies. This is for two hours every day. They pump in pressurized oxygen that you breathe to help your body begin to heal from the inside out. These chambers are used for deep sea divers that come up too quickly. They call the two hour process a "Dive." I was told I would probably need 20 to 30 dives and my foot should be healed. After 30 dives I was told we should try 20 or 30 more. After 30 more I was told...well let's move forward. I did 100 dives, a record I was told. I thought I was going to get a plaque or a trophy or maybe they would name one of the chambers after me but my infection was still there. At this point the bright side of things was getting pretty dim. I was never claustrophobic but the more dives I did the more it felt like torture. If I was ever a POW this is one way they could get me to talk.

There were a few times the infection got so bad my wife had to rush me to the hospital for a two or three day visit. The last visit to the hospital, my doctor announced that we could start all over – or amputate below the knee. I thought about the things I used to do, the things I still wanted to do, the things

I wasn't able to do in the previous two years. I thought about losing a part of my body and how I could crack the knuckle on my right big toe by just bending it. I thought about all I'd been through and all my family and friends had been through to help me heal. I thought about the pain and the looks I'd get only having one leg. I wondered if I would ever be able to drive again and how important that has always been to me. What if they botch the amputation and it becomes worse? What if the insurance company said they've had enough and I'm on my own? I'm not a gambler. I felt like I was given a choice to jump out a ten story window into a small cup of water or swim a mile under water holding my breath.

"Let's do it," I said.

I got everything in order and the night before returning to the hospital my wife and I went to "The last Supper" at an Italian restaurant. I was now ready. I returned to the hospital and was quickly and effectively relieved of twelve pounds of weight, which I was always working to lose but not like this. I stayed about three days and returned home thinking everything was going to be ok. Then all of a sudden, about a week later, I was back in the hospital. My leg got an infection completely unrelated to the foot.

Back to the hospital I went and stayed for two and a half weeks. At this point I began to get angry, and from frustration found myself yelling at my wife. It felt like I would never kick this infection, almost like I was circling the drain so to speak. I was starting to believe there was no bright side left and I was losing this battle. I needed to convince myself it was just another speed bump even though it looked like another mountain to climb.

Maybe, if I could surround myself with some familiar things from home I would be more comfortable. So I asked my wife to bring my satellite radio and my head phones. Since they let me bring those in, I might as well bring my guitar and small amplifier so that I could plug in my headphones.

I was being operated on every other day. It was operation day, recovery day, operation day, recovery day, on and on for two and a half weeks. I asked why I needed to wear that thin smock with the ties on the back and nothing underneath when I'm not operated on. I know it's a good look and oh so comfortable on a big guy like me, but I was thinking about everyone around me. So they said I could actually wear my shorts and a tee shirt, and allowed me to go up to the roof on the sixth floor with my guitar and hang out in the sun.

Two and a half weeks went by very slowly, but the day finally came when I was infection free and my leg was closed back up and I could go home. I did everything but get up on my one good leg and hop out of there.

I was finally home and feeling good. I just needed to heal but I was in a wheel chair. I'm a driver. If I can either fly somewhere or drive, I drive. Whenever I'm in a car with other people, ninety-nine times out of hundred, I'm driving. I wasn't sure I could go four months without being behind the wheel even for freedom's sake. I put a bumper rack on the back of my Jeep which held my wheelchair. I would wheel myself out to the Jeep, take my walker out of the back, hold myself up with the walker and then put the wheelchair on the rack. I would then hobble around to the driver's side and fold up the walker, get in and drive with my left foot. This by the way was evaluated and approved by my wife who made me demonstrate that I could do all of this safely. But it worked! It had to. And it worked for four months. I could go to doctor appointments, meet friends for lunch, go down to the beach and wheel myself around. I made it work.

After the four months of doctor's appointments and therapy sessions they cleared me for a prosthesis. One thing I found through this whole adventure was that the insurance company was fantastic. Yes, you read right. I'm not a fan of insurance companies. You're basically betting them that you will get into an accident and they're betting you won't. You are betting against yourself. In this case I guess I won so off to the Prostheticist I went.

He made molds of my stump, took measurements, showed me different types of legs and feet. A few weeks went by and I finally got the call to come in and pick up my new leg. My wife followed me with camera in hand. I was overwhelmed with the suspension sleeves and gel liners, carbon fiber sockets and titanium pylons. As he fitted me with my new leg I was already looking forward to when my stump would be atrophied enough to get a second one. I also thought about what people would think – for only about five seconds. Living in Southern California, I like to wear shorts and one could not miss the fact that my legs look different. Being a car collector I thought it would break the ice if I put hot rod flames on my leg. I found a place online that sold stick-on flames of all sizes. So on the flames went, and not only did they break the ice, they melted it to the point of people not turning away, and me even making some new friends. They noticed it wasn't a touchy subject.

Three months later I was back for another fitting and shortly after I received my second leg, I developed a problem with showering. You can't use your normal prosthetic leg to shower. There are things that can't get wet so they made me a shower leg. But I like to swim and I found out you can't swim with a shower leg because you can't point your toes. So they made me a swim leg with a button release on the ankle so I can point my toes and swim. I then saw an ad for a hydraulic ankle. It allows the foot to point the toe down as you take a step and to point up as you follow through. So they made me one with a hydraulic ankle. What a wonderful piece of heaven this thing is. With long pants on you can't tell I'm a "monoped."

Two years after losing my leg I'm still looking at the bright side of things. You have to. Through this whole journey my grandkids have been way too helpful. I say "way too helpful" because there are things I don't ask of them, they just do. My wife has been very supportive and was always by my side through this whole affair. She even makes fun of me when I do dumb stuff like stand up forgetting that my leg isn't on. I always have the sensation that my leg is still there so I have to be careful. Sometimes my removed foot actually itches and I have the sensation that I can wiggle my toes. Whenever I drive my wife's car I literally feel a cool breeze flowing through my absent toes as if the floor vent is open.

The prostheticist is the best. He not only knows what he's doing but we've really connected on a personal level and that helps when I ask him about a new technology. The insurance company, which has never said no, is always there for me. All the people in the hospital and the wound center, where I did my hyperbaric treatments, have been wonderful, dedicated people. The fact is that I'm healthy again, and we can no longer joke about it "being a nightmare." Through this adventure I was never in any real pain for any length of time.

Whenever I hear people complain about doctors or the people at the grocery store, airlines or just everyday interactions, I remember some things I learned on my sixty trips around the sun. You get out of a situation what you bring to it. If you have a positive attitude you will receive positive things in return. Also be the captain of your ship. If someone wants you to wear a skimpy smock with an open back and you are uncomfortable, say something. You are the one who sets your course. If you happen to sail into a storm and you are prepared, you'll make it out the other end. Don't panic. I've done everything I could through this storm, and in turn the doctors and the insurance company have done everything they could do also. I still look at the positive side of life. When people tell me that they are sorry about my leg and it must be difficult with just one, I remind them I have one good leg and five prosthetic ones. I am a six legged man!

Mike Senzamici lives in Santa Barbara California with his wife Robin. He is a Vintage Car Collector and also enjoys playing guitar and banjo. For fun he plays in a band called "The Seven Foot String Band" and goes to Vintage Camper Meets in their restored 1948 Greyhound bus.

WHAT HAPPENED TO YOUR EYE?

David H. Barnhouse, M.D.

Some forty or fifty years ago, while I was doing my residency in general surgery in Rochester, N. Y., Dr. George Emerson, thoracic surgeon at the University Hospital, showed up one Monday morning with a very black eye. I saw him several times during that busy day, either in the operating suite, or making rounds on the wards. At last my curiosity overcame my respect and awe for this great surgeon, and I timidly asked, "Um, uh, Dr. Emerson, what happened to …" He pulled a three by five card from his pocket and smilingly handed it to me before I could finish saying, "… your eye?" As I read the few lines saying that he had fallen and hit his eye on a branch while skiing, he continued to smile, and said, "David, I knew that everyone I saw today would ask that question, so I typed up this card." We both laughed.

Maybe I'll just follow his example but improve on it a bit, I thought, because I have managed to come up with a similar appearance this week. But instead of typing up a card, I've decided to write this essay you are reading. And by the way, I am curious as to how these black and blue circles around my eye got to be called 'shiners'. Wouldn't a better word be 'dullers'?

You'd think that after fifty-eight years Mary Alice would know that my attention to others was no possible threat to her. But she found my friendliness with some of the Q-tips at our retirement home a little excessive, so she made her point with her fist. You may ask, "Q-tips?" Oh, we call Q-tips the tiny old ladies with white hair.

No, what really happened was this. I was walking up our Main Street late one Friday evening, when I came upon some teen-agers bullying a little kid. Foolishly, I waded in, and suggested that they pick on someone their own size. "OK, wise guy!" and they turned on me. "You're about my size, so here's to you!" Before I could either duck, or raise my arms, one of those ruffians lashed out and landed one on my eye. Then they ran off.

If you think that explanation is a little unlikely, and that this staid old geezer would really never have been foolish enough to interfere in such a situation . . . Well then, how about this explanation: It was Friday evening all right, but instead of walking down Main Street, I was sitting in a bar with the most recent of several beers that I had been unsuccessfully nursing to overcome my anxieties about the upcoming elections. What if the Tea Party and the Koen brothers had really bought the election? Would Texas money really be able to take over California? Was the USA doomed to become an empire with the rich being wealthy at the expense of the ever increasing number of poor? Was the middle class really going to disappear?

All of a sudden, a man further down the bar proclaimed loudly that he hoped the new government would plant land mines every three feet along the entire Mexican border. Astounded and appalled, I jumped up and said, "You sound just like Adolph Hitler!" His response? He gave me this souvenir....

Am I still seeing some raised eyebrows among you? Would an aged Episcopal priest be that drunk, that stupid or both? Well then, maybe I should get closer to the truth. I live in a retirement home. When we arrived here, I became acquainted with many of the three or four hundred residents. I have recently been surprised at the appearance of the men and women who sit down in the dining room each night. Many are using canes or walkers now. In contrast to Mary Alice and me, they look a great deal older than they did eight years ago.

Twice a week I take an hour's balance class in an effort to keep myself from falling. I find this an important precaution against the dangerous risk that old people face. Well, I am sorry to report that in spite of all precautions, I tripped while walking from the dining hall on that Friday night, and I banged my head against a door stop. Fortunately the balance class had taught me how to protect my limbs while falling. This way, I hit my eye without breaking a hip....

A minute ago I used the words "closer to the truth." Somewhere in the back of my alleged mind, a little gremlin is reminding me that truth is not really arbitrary. Something is either true or false. It can't be close.

All right then, see what you think of this story. Of course, you are free to consider any of the five earlier explanations, but here's another one. About a month ago I noticed a slightly tender lump in my eyelid, and Mary Alice convinced me that I should go see an eye doctor. He put me on the table, stabbed it and sucked out some oil. He told me it was probably a chalazion, a condition caused by an obstructed oil gland. I asked him if BP, as careless as they had been with oil in the Gulf of Mexico, might be responsible, and would he please then send them the bill. Later, the doctor told me that instead of spilling oil, BP had blocked the outlet severely enough that he wanted to biopsy it.

Once more to the table, and this time he injected some local anesthesia and started to dig around in my eyelid with what felt like an axe and pick. In what seemed like about ten hours, he had finished, and I was able to go home. However, my souvenir for my trouble, appeared in a day or two. It was this shiner, or rather, this duller. Like on some beaches, you see the results of oil problems. Same here.

The next big question concerns the results of the biopsy. Don't medical terms have an appealing, poetic, or onomatopoeic sound? Think of mellifluous words like amblyopia, rhabdomyoliposarcoma, mesothelioma, or oligodendroglioma. But, I didn't rate one of those. All the drama I was offered was 'Benign cyst.'

There you are. Take your pick. But I do ask that you not pity me. Just laugh.

I practiced surgery and urology in India, and Pittsburgh, PA. Having been active in spiritual matters, I decided to become a priest in the Episcopal tradition when I retired from the medical field. In 2002, my wife and I moved to the Samarkand, a retirement community in Santa Barbara, CA.

LOVE IN THE TIME OF DEMENTIA

Vivian Browne

My children don't like to ask. But I can see it in their eyes: They have heard stories......

When visiting me in my new Assisted Living facility – "Welcome to New Life Valley of the Dolls," it said (*a little colored pill for everything that ails you; or irks the staff*) – they want to know if I am having sex.

To ease their discomfort, I tell them a classic nursing home joke: the one about the elderly woman who would visit her love interest every afternoon......

They would sit for hours together, with her hand resting on his penis. One day she showed up at their regular time only to find he wasn't there. Fearing the worst, she contacted the floor's nurse wondering what had become of him. The nurse explained that he was fine but she had seen him with another woman.

The next day the woman confronted her love interest and questioned him about this other woman. She wondered how he could leave her after all the intimate afternoons spent together with her hand on his manhood.

"Name me one thing she has that I don't?" she asked.

He looked at her and answered…. "Parkinsons…."

My children wriggle uncomfortably in their wicker visiting seats but giggling slightly, feel freer to inquire "What about you Mom?"

I tell them that unfortunately, since I don't have Parkinson's, I am less in demand, but that, yes, indeed I do have a few gentlemen callers. I quickly add, before they have a chance to fully digest the significance of this, that they should be grateful because I am doing this for their benefit.

"What!" they cry.

"Yes," I say, "I have read about a Canadian study that found that sex burns fat and causes the brain to release endorphins that act as painkillers and reduce anxiety. And, not only that, sex also seems to prompt the release of substances that bolster the immune system…

"So, just think of all the money I am saving you on additional medications!"

I do not add that the same study also said that sex about three times a week can slow aging and prevent wrinkles around the eyes. Really!

"Besides," I say, "I am helping out the staff. They were complaining to me about being groped and fondled - and I am much more experienced at handling those situations than they are.

"In fact they should pay me for my services. Perhaps I'll organize the 'inmates' – and save you even more money - by earning some of my own!"

(*I did not mention that I had actually heard about a nursing home in England that was hiring "sex workers" – prostitutes - who meet residents in a designated room and put a "special red sock" on the door for privacy. A spokesperson told the press that Professionals offer a service that is both therapeutic to residents frustrated by 'primeval needs' and helpful for the staff).*

Of course, that idea takes care of the male residents. But my new 'business venture' would be a win-win for both sexes!

"I wonder if Medicare would reimburse?" I add out loud.

"Mom, be serious" they say. "What is really going on with you? Do you have a boyfriend?"

"Not yet," I say. "I am testing the waters. As the new game in town, I am pretty popular at the moment."

I could not tell them that this popularity had already cost me a few female friends. When I first arrived, several women had 'approached' me to 'warn me off' of their "boyfriends." The competition for men around here is pretty fierce. Any man, it seems!

"And, besides," I say, "since I have people to do my laundry for me, I don't have to cook and am not much for card-playing or TV – so, aside from bingo, what else is there to do?"

(Aah.... that just gave me another idea: strip poker. A game likely to take up the whole evening, considering all the undergarments to be removed).

"You know, in the nursing home adjacent to this facility, they are required to keep the doors open at night – and the staff tells me that several of the men masturbate practically all night long. They think there is the added incentive of being watched. Perhaps they were flashers in their previous lives!" I joke, trying to deflect the conversation away from me just a little bit.

It worked!

My son chimes in: "I have a nursing home-flasher joke.... So a couple of little old ladies were sitting outside one day when a flasher did his thing right in front of them. The first one had a stroke. The second one had a stroke. The third didn't. Her arms were too short and she couldn't reach."

"That's awful" says my daughter, laughing.

"Why are old ladies always 'little' in jokes? I'm still quite tall," was the only comment I had to make.

"How are the kids?" I ask referring to my three grandchildren, aged 13, 16 and 18.

"They're fine," my daughter, responsible for two of them replies, "and planning to come visit you very soon."

"You know how they make sure that they get visits from their grandchildren here?" I ask. "They send checks for birthdays and holidays – and they don't sign them. They know the grandkids will assume they just forgot!" This time, it was only me who chuckled.

Later, I contemplated our conversation – and their curiosity about my sex life. Why is it that we can never imagine our parents having sex? And, our grandparents? Yuk! And, when they're over 80? Yuk! Yuk!

Realizing this, and to '*reassure*' them, just before they left, I reminded them, "Don't forget to bring condoms on your next visit. That will prevent the spread of any sexually transmitted diseases amongst us old folks that you have been hearing so much about in the news." (*But, really, the news is about much younger 'old folks' – those summer of love 'Baby Boomers' - of whom there are not yet that many living in places like this*).

"I will ask the staff to hand them out with the Viagra!"

They do not answer.

Interestingly, I noted, they never really asked about love and affection. Here at New Life Valley (of the Knolls, not Dolls) there are more than a few couples: some who came in that way; some who have found each other here. They are soulmates – and sexmates. And, despite all the jokes about the advantages of poor eyesight and not being able to remember if, or how many times, they might have had sex on a given night (or day), seeing them together has been heartwarming to me, and gives me hope for my own future. Something to look forward to – even now.

Yet I know there are many facilities that seek to control personal contact between residents, often because of their own legal vulnerability - but also out of concern for the safety of those residents. It is a complicated issue, but one that might be partially addressed by a sexual – as well as a medical – advance directive or living will.

But, hopefully, always addressed with some humor.

And compassion.

After all, at our age, why not?

Vivian Browne is a senior whose need is to view the world lightly – albeit in a somewhat quirky way. "Otherwise," she says, "we would all go crazy." The story was specifically written for LTCRW – a commission to write about the reality of life in a Retirement or Nursing Home. This is her version of that 'reality.'

PART 2

Don't Overlook The Obvious

"Life is not a journey to the grave with the intention of arriving safely in a pretty and well preserved body, but rather to skid in broadside, thoroughly used up, totally worn out and loudly proclaiming, 'Wow, what a ride!'"

Unknown

IT'S NEVER TOO LATE FOR ADVENTURE

Judith Geller

Remember the game we played in childhood, where you would be asked to fall backwards and trust that someone would catch you? I was never able to do that. Yet here I am in my sunset years, trusting a complete stranger with my life.

Zac Majors, a national hang gliding champion who certifies people to become tandem hang gliding teachers is my "stranger." The minute I meet him, seeing his calm and happy persona, I intuitively know he is someone I can trust. Zac tells me he only certifies people he would let his mother ride with. "Of course," he adds laughing, "my mother won't even ride with me!"

I have never been an athletic person because I have always been nervous about getting hurt. I know how to swim, ski and dance, but I have never been interested in anything fast or intense like bungee jumping or skydiving. For some strange, unknown reason, I have always wanted to hang glide, to float in the air like a bird, to know what it's like to be free of the heaviness of the body.

Zac and I drive up three thousand feet above sea level to the top of a launch site called the Skyport. I tell Zac that my main fear is that on landing I will twist an ankle or break a leg so that I won't be able to dance, a passion I engage in at least twice a week. However, I am determined to follow his directions and not get caught in the endless questions arising from my fear.

As this enormous glider, with a thirty-four foot wing span, is being set up, I sign the necessary release forms and listen to Zac's instructions. Then I practice running alongside Zac up and down the road several times. "Be sure you stay close and lean into me," he says.

Zac helps me suit up, hooks me to the center of the glider and checks that everything is in order. Then he rolls the glider into position for takeoff. About to jump off the cliff, I am extremely nervous. Because of all the instructions, I am under the impression we are going to start about ten feet back and run to the cliff's edge, but clearly this is not the plan. Zac pulls the glider right up to the edge of the precipice.

"Judy, What I am going to ask you is, 'Are you ready,' and I want to hear you say 'yes' loud and clear. When I yell, 'run' be sure to look at the Island across the channel. Do you understand?"

"Yes." I nod. I know that there is no way I can look down 3,000 feet without freaking out. I have to focus on the distant island. Nervously, I ask, "What foot do you start on?"

"I think I start on my left," he replies, "but it doesn't matter." Still with my dancer's mentality, it matters to me.

"Okay, here we go. Are you ready Judy?"

"Yes," I say loudly.

But then, suddenly, we don't move.

Zac tells me he's waiting for a thermal…" We wait: It feels like forever. The thermal comes and goes. "I am waiting for another one. Okay now… Are you ready?" he asks again.

"Yes," I say more feebly.

"Clear… now RUN!"

I focus intensely on the distant island, and after taking only a single step on land, I am already flying. Of course it doesn't matter what foot I start on, since I find myself now running in the air. Immediately, all the fear falls away.

I am just present, happy and gliding like a bird ever so easily over beautiful estates, lush mountains, trees and fields. In the distance is the ocean covered with downy white clouds. There is a gentle breeze on my face as I float weightlessly through the air. I feel secure with Zac next to me and follow his suggestion to put my hands on the bar so that for a few minutes I can steer the glider. Surrounded by beauty, peace and quiet, it suddenly occurs to me that this is one more way to dance.

After about fifteen minutes, Zac says that it is time to land and he explains, "We can do one of two things now, Judy. We can do some circles and maneuvers in the air first or we can just have a nice smooth landing. It's your choice."

"I'll take the nice smooth landing," I reply with a grateful smile.

"That's good," Zac says. "Then we can have more time in the air."

A short while later, he tells me we will be landing soon and to follow his instructions. I look down at the ground that appears to be coming up way too fast. I hear Zac say, 'Start running now!' so I start wildly moving my legs like a sprinter through the air. The next thing I know, before I can even feel my fear, we're seated together on the ground laughing. It was so quick, so easy, so gentle.

Feeling exhilarated sitting next to Zac, I am amazed that I've been able to transcend my fear and stay present throughout this experience. This shows me it is never too late for adventure. With openness and trust, you can fly at any age!

Judith Geller has been a model, actress, singer, and composer/lyricist. She is now a writer and editor.

YOU JUST DON'T LISTEN

Jack Malken

YOU JUST DON'T LISTEN, DO YOU? THAT'S RIGHT! I DON'T.

I committed the cardinal sin... I did it. I... wrote a... wait for it... here it comes... a screenplay. At the age of 62, OOh nooooo.

"Everyone has written a screenplay including my Grandmother."

"Selling a screenplay is like hitting the lottery!"

"Hollywood will tear you apart."

"I've heard that exact same story before."

These are the encouraging words I've heard from almost everyone. All of it fell on deaf ears, because, I DON'T LISTEN! Since kindergarten, then on through high school, except for my father, I don't remember getting any encouragement from anyone.

While attending college, I announced that I wanted to go into the music business. My mother and brother were the most pessimistic. "You have no talent." "You have no connections." "You're gonna starve!" Okay, but at 19 I signed a major record deal for my group with Warner Brothers Records, by 27

I wrote, played and recorded hit records and by 30 opened my own recording studio and independent record label. I owned a rock music club and modeling agency and that was all before I turned 50 and retired.

After retiring and being bored to tears, something happened. I started to experience a burst, an explosion really, of energy and inspirational creativity resulting in three movie scripts and twelve brand new songs for a CD. I even found myself with a strong renewed activist concern for the future existence of our planet, our civilization and society, and an overwhelming desire to actively participate in whatever cures may be available.

But this is about after I turned 60. I can still recall the constant refrain, "You just don't listen!" It's true, I don't and never have. I don't listen to any one that tells me I can't do something, or I will fail miserably.

So I started writing my movie script at the tender age of fifty-nine and finally made a deal for one screenplay at sixty-three. It is in development right now. I am one of those that believe your age is not something you have any control over, so why worry about it. I figure in another ten year's science will have discovered a cure for death!

I can still hear the classic putdowns: "Are you NUTZ, totally out of your mind?" "Don't quit your day job!" "It will never work." "If it's so good, why hasn't someone else done it?" "At your age?" And those were the people trying to *help* with their great advice. Ever heard any of these? Of course you have. You know the age old saying "If I had a nickel for every time someone tried to discourage me, I would have a million dollars' worth of nickels."

It took four years and three computers (two wore out) before I finished. *Yes*, I did finish my screenplay including umpteen rewrites. Now please, let me define finished. In Hollywoodese it means I have written enough words, based on a strong story idea, to give to someone else, (usually a few someone elses) to rewrite it into something exactly the same, only different. If that makes any sense to you, you have a great future as a movie executive. It is true (someone showed me the math), that there are over a million screenplays in circulation, for sale, at any given moment. That gives anyone who is not personally related to James Cameron or Steven Spielberg less chance than getting hit by lightning.

The secret to great writing is: say it elegantly, be brief, and stay as close to the point as possible. Ooops, I broke that one already. The screenplay I wrote is not about four people sitting around a dinner table discussing issues regarding family, career, politics, or life. It is, in fact, what is known in the film industry as a High Concept, Tent Pole, Sci-Fi, Gigantic Budget (128 mil), Apocalyptic, Action Adventure, Epic. It addresses a burning issue: For every action there is a re-action. What possible consequences could there be as we suck every drop of oil out of the Earth? One possibility is that the Earth starts to warm up, break up, lose gravity and finally collapses and disintegrates in earthquakes and volcanic eruptions. The less oil within our planet, the more frequent and violent the earthquakes.

Some thought it was a crazy idea until I found existing research that supported it.

I believe that it is crucial right now for all of us NOT TO LISTEN to the mass retail communications that pass for news in our daily lives. Most of what we are exposed to is more like a reality show than real, objective, honest news reporting. We must seek out sources for honest, truthful information so that we can decide for ourselves what is important on a global stage. We cannot hide our heads in the sand and hope all the boogiemen go away.

The more I researched, the deeper I got into the science, and the more anxious I became. My initial concept was supported by the increasing research and proving to be correct.

At this point I just hope my movie comes out ... before it has a chance to be proven true.

But, I've also never listened to those that say "our country is going to pot" (which may not be so bad), "the younger generation is no good" and "vinyl records will never come back".

In short, I tend to have a positive outlook on life. Why not? You might as well have a smile on your face as the whole world comes to a crashing end.

The moral of my story: unless you're about to be hit by a bus and someone is trying to warn you... DON'T LISTEN!

Raised to be a Rabbi with dreams of being a Rock Star, Jack Malken settled for Hollywood and making movies. His path was as straight and true as the steel ball in an old time pinball machine. From Yeshiva to Public High School to Greenwich Village to California, bumping into the Ramones, Bette Midler, Todd Rundgren, and others along the way. Every ten years have been the best ten years of his life.

WISING UP

Milton Teichman

Gary Feld, approaching eighty, was proud of his youthfulness. In the gym, he lifted weights four times a week and then swam twenty-five laps. On the three remaining days of the week, he walked two miles with his wife Ruth on the bike trail behind their house on Cape Cod. Gary knew of friends and acquaintances who were younger, who rested during the afternoon, or who fell asleep watching television in the evening. But for Gary, life was too interesting to spend time napping.

After forty-seven years of teaching English on the college level, Gary retired and devoted himself to making art. What had earlier been a passionate avocation now became his daily work – work that made him feel young. When he was painting in his studio or making sculptures in his workshop, he felt he was engaged in wondrous play. 'To make something with my hands,' he said to himself, 'is to feel young.'

During the winters he and Ruth spent in Mexico, he not only made art, he also wrote stories. A few were already published, and he decided that soon he would gather a dozen together to form a book, even if he had to publish it himself. It was not recognition he wanted, just a reinforcement of the pleasure he had in creating something that didn't exist before – and perhaps a little validation. Moving toward eighty was not so bad after all, he thought.

"You seem so tired after your workouts," Ruth said to him one afternoon while he was looking through the newspaper. "Don't you think you should take it a little easier?"

"Nonsense," he replied, his pride slightly injured. "How will I know I'm exercising if I don't *feel* it?" He noticed he was mouthing what he'd overheard students saying to one another.

"I just think you're overdoing it. Be careful, dear."

There were signs of getting older that Gary couldn't deny. He could not walk up or down a flight of stairs as easily as he could in the past. His tolerance for winter cold was diminishing, and the hilly streets in the Mexican town where he and Ruth spent the winter, sometimes left him out of breath. But he was proud of the fact that he was still slender and weighed only slightly more than he did when he entered college. And he was grateful that he was free of serious medical problems—free of the medical blows that were overwhelming friends and acquaintances.

He recalled that by the time his parents reached seventy, they had already struggled with chronic infirmities. Surely, he was not immune to the physical and mental stresses time can bring. Yes, he still enjoyed good health. But what if he suddenly became ill while in Mexico—far from familiar doctors and hospitals? He wondered whether he and Ruth should buy insurance that would speed them home from Mexico should they have a medical emergency. He tried to dispel such disquieting thoughts. 'It's not like me to think this way,' he thought to himself. 'Didn't the Bible say that Moses lived until one hundred twenty—with vigor?' But then he thought of the patriarch Isaac who went blind in his old age, and of aged Job who suffered physical and mental agonies beyond counting. 'No,' he told himself, 'I won't let my thoughts go in that direction.'

⁌

Gary was not enthusiastic about accepting the dinner invitation he and Ruth received from Nancy and Fred Berger. Gary found Fred's conversation filled with indiscretions, clichés, and complaints about his physical distresses. He found these complaints, tedious – and a bit unnerving.

"It's a different ailment each year," he complained to Ruth.

"Why are you being so critical and fault-finding?" For a moment, Gary felt the sting of her words, and his resolve to turn down the social invitation weakened.

A blanket of late December snow covered the lawn and low shrubs in front of the Berger's home. Fred and Nancy greeted them so warmly upon their arrival that Gary wondered again whether he was too severe in his previous judgments.

"We're going to miss you folks," said Nancy. "Three winter months in Mexico. What lucky people you are."

"Yes, we are lucky," Gary replied. "But I don't have to tell you that travel today is no picnic—there's getting to the airport in Boston from the Cape, the baggage inspections; and though I like walking, there's so much walking in huge airports it's like an endurance test."

"Still, you're mighty lucky people," said Fred.

Ruth and Gary were ushered from the entry hall to the living room and were presented with an array of pre-dinner snacks.

Gary noticed that Fred was limping. He was about to inquire about the limp when Fred asked, "Don't you guys worry about the crime in Mexico? The papers are full of it."

"You're thinking of the border with the U.S. It's not bad at all in southern Mexico where we stay," Gary answered.

"Well, that's good. Glad to know you guys are safe."

Ruth excused herself to offer help to Nancy in the kitchen. As Fred sat down across from Gary, he winced in response to the pain in his leg.

"I see that knee of yours is giving you trouble."

"If it's not one thing, it's another. This bum knee makes me feel like a really old guy." Fred sighed audibly. "You know, before we know it, we fall apart. That's what happens to us. We simply fall apart…"

Gary wondered how he could get off this conversation when Fred said, "So what's new with you?"

"The usual things, painting, finishing a wood sculpture, a bit of writing, exercising each morning — and now a hundred details before we leave for Mexico."

The dinner Nancy served was superlative.

"Fred and I will be spending February in Sarasota again," Nancy announced. "We rented a condo close to the beach."

"I used to love winter," Fred said, "but all I need now is to slip on snow or ice and I'm done for . . . But we find Sarasota is damn expensive! Like you, we'd prefer to spend three months of the winter in Mexico or maybe in South America where it's reasonable. But if we'd have some medical emergency, we'd be thousands of miles from home. Why take the chance?"

Gary and Ruth glanced at each other, nodded, but made no reply.

Fred hobbled about the dinner table filling glasses with after-dinner drinks. 'Given his bad knee,' Gary thought, 'it's good of him to make this effort at entertaining.'

There was a lull in the conversation when Nancy asked, "So when do you people actually leave for Mexico?"

"The first of January," answered Ruth, "if God is willing."

"Oh, you don't believe in that God-stuff!" Fred exclaimed with a sweep of his arm.

With a mischievous grin, Gary said, "I'll give you another version, Fred. We leave on the first of January, *if the creek don't rise.*"

This levity did not last long because Fred turned back to the subject of his accumulating ailments.

"I wonder," Ruth said, "why we don't talk more about what we gain as we get older—a deeper feeling for loved ones and friends, more clarity about what's important in life, and therefore more clarity about how best to use our time."

Gary looked over at his wife. A sense of admiration warmed him.

"And what about gratitude?" she went on. "For those of us with fair health and reasonable financial security, isn't there a fuller sense than before of appreciation, a sense that with every birthday – no, with every day – we are given a gift of time?"

Ruth stopped, as though a little surprised at the animated way she was expressing herself. Meanwhile, Gary was so moved by what his wife was saying that he felt a sudden rush of love toward her and even an overflow of warm feeling toward Fred and Nancy. He felt like adding something personal about himself and even sharing some of his own deep feelings. He looked at Fred and Nancy, hesitated, and then obeyed his impulse.

"Can I share something with you, folks?" he began. He felt a strong urge to enlarge on Ruth's words, to speak from his own experiences on this subject. "I'm going to be eighty in a few months, and I want to say…"

Gary would have finished his sentence except that Fred, with a broad grin on his face, burst out, "Eighty? Why, you're an old fart!"

Stunned, Gary felt as if a massive wall were suddenly thrust in front of him. Fred's words were icy stabs. 'How could he say that to me?' Gary thought. 'Does he know who he's talking to?' In a stern and demanding voice, as though about to rebuke an insolent student, he replied, "I want you to revise what you just said."

Fred's jaw dropped. He looked confused. He gave short, uncertain glances around the room.

"Come on now," said Gary firmly. "I want you to modify what you just said."

Still bewildered, Fred answered, "Okay, do you want me to say that you're now a golden-ager, or something like that?"

"You're making things worse, Fred," and still fixing his eyes on his host he said, "I have to tell you something about yourself: There's not an idea or sentiment of any value that you don't flatten out or trivialize." Saying these words, Gary felt a momentary flush of satisfaction.

Fred sat stunned, robbed of speech. Ruth hesitated, not knowing whether she should intervene.

Breaking the silence, Nancy spoke up, "You're taking it all too personally, Gary. Fred's just joking. Can't you tell? He's really talking about himself."

"Well, let him admit that," said Gary. And staring at Fred, who had an uncomprehending look on his face, he added, "I find his crudeness more than I can take."

"But that's his charm," replied Nancy. "Haven't you noticed?"

"Not to me!" Gary declared, and he continued to feel the hurt of Fred's remark.

Ruth hoped that Fred would speak up, to offer some apology, even if only a pale one for offending Gary, or that Nancy would make some apology for her husband. In that way, maybe the evening could be salvaged.

Gary could not control his upset. He rose from the dinner table, turned to Ruth and announced, "I'm uncomfortable here. It's time for us to leave."

Though shaken, Ruth thanked Nancy for the beautiful meal and expressed regret that things turned out the way they did. Gary wanted to get out of their home as quickly as he could. He feigned a civility he did not feel: "Have a good winter," he said to both of them, looking neither of them in the eyes. "Enjoy Florida."

"I've never had an encounter like this in my entire life," Gary declared on the drive home. Ruth cautioned him to watch for icy patches on the road. "My God! To insult a guest you bring into your home. Not to say you're sorry for offending." Ruth listened silently wondering what she could say to ease her husband's distress.

When they reached home, Gary felt strangely chilled. "I'm shivering. I'd better put on something warm," he said checking the thermostat. He returned with a jacket.

"Come, Gary...We've been jarred by the experience. Let's sit on the couch together for a while and calm ourselves."

"What's wrong with me, Ruth? Why am I reacting so strongly?"

⌒

It happened that during their stay in Oaxaca, Mexico, many of the old streets and sidewalks were being torn up and resurfaced. On his walk home from the ceramics studio one evening, Gary had to walk around a piece of paving equipment that was in his path. He lost his balance and fell. He took a clean handkerchief from his pocket and gently dabbed the bleeding wound on his right knee.

"I guess I just lost my balance," he explained to Ruth later as she helped to clean the wound and apply a bandage. Maybe I should do some exercise to improve my balance."

'Rather than a new exercise program', Ruth thought, 'Gary should see a doctor.' Then she said to Gary, "This cut looks deep and might need stitches."

"Maybe you're right," he said. And with a worried look, he added, "It was an oversight not to identify a doctor in the neighborhood in advance. Emergencies happen."

"It's hard to think of everything," she answered, and she applied a fresh bandage to the wound.

After a few days of discomfort, Gary was back on his feet again. But his fall, and his sense that his balance was off, had a sobering effect on him. He could not put aside his fears — fears of possible future disability and pain, declining strength, dependency on others. He imagined himself infirm and a daily burden to Ruth. 'I've not prepared myself enough for the future,' he thought, and he chided himself for avoiding reality.

"I think I've unwittingly slipped into the culture's obsession with youth.'

Some days afterward when he and Ruth were walking home after having dinner at a restaurant facing the colorful city square, he shared his apprehensions with her.

"I haven't heard you speak of these matters before," she said.

"Maybe I've been a bit scared to face them."

"It's good that you can talk about them now." She took hold of his hand. "We all have to strike a good balance between optimism and realism," she added. "I think I happen to lean in your direction, so your thoughts are helping me too."

"And one more thing, Ruth... I've been thinking... Do you believe another person in my place would have reacted to Fred in the same way I did when we were at the Burger's?" And before she could answer, he added, "It's unlikely, isn't it?"

⁓

At first, Gary was reluctant to have a birthday party with attention focused entirely on him, but in the end he gave way to Ruth's urgings. "It's not just any birthday. It's your eightieth."

The party took place in their home on Cape Cod, where friends could see Gary's new art work. They offered many toasts in his honor.

"Let's have some words from the young man," asked one of the guests. Other guests echoed the request. "Yes, some words, a speech from the young man."

This is just what he wanted to avoid, but his embarrassment lessened when he thought to himself that all he needed to say was "Thank you." He could be brief.

"Thank you all for coming," he began. "Thank you for friendship. Thank you, Ruth, for being my spiritual twin and the blessing of my life." He paused, swallowed, and felt strong feeling rising up in him. "And thank God for the gift of time I've received—eighty years—full of friendship and love, and a chance to express my modest abilities."

"Congratulations!" "Good health!" "Until one hundred and twenty!" came the chorus of replies. Gary thought he'd stop speaking at this point. He had said "Thank you," but something moved him to continue.

"You asked a 'young man' to say some words. Well, I'm young in *here*." And he pointed to his head. "And I'm young in *here*," and he pointed to his heart" He paused for a moment. "But the calendar tells its truth too. I'm really an old man. As someone said to me recently, "At eighty, you're an old fart." A burst of laughter came from the group. "At seventy, I used to tell people that I was in my 'advanced youth,' but that's not the truth now, because the body's messages are getting clearer, and I expect they'll be getting clearer still."

He paused, looked around at his guests, and then met the gaze of Ruth standing at the far end of the room.

"Let me say what may surprise you. I know the coming years have to go down-hill. I saw it in my elderly parents, and many of you saw it in your parents as well." But saying this, an old fear gripped him, and he had to stop to calm himself.

The room fell silent. All eyes were on him.

He wished he could end his talk right there. The party was a mistake. He should not have agreed to it. And yet something compelled him to go on. "If trouble down the road is a sure thing," he continued haltingly, "what can we do about it? I know what I must do—accept what can't be changed, face whatever comes with courage, and feel gratitude for what has been."

A hum of affirmation and agreement sounded in the room. "There's a wise man for you," someone called out loudly.

"And not only feel gratitude for what has been but for what remains." He could hear the unsteadiness in his voice. "We don't lose our capacity to love and be loved," Gary went on, then looking over at Ruth. She smiled at him and gave him an encouraging nod. "The creative abilities we all have do not dry up." He paused again. "If we get our cataracts removed," he smiled, "we can see even more of the beauty around us. And the ordinary and the familiar can still fill us with wonder."

Applause and cheers filled the room. Gary shook many hands and gave and received many hugs. Ruth stepped forward to embrace her husband.

Several days later, Gary said to Ruth, "I've been thinking . . . I have some unfinished business."

He picked up the phone and dialed Fred's number.

Milton Teichman is a writer, educator, and visual artist. He is editor (with Sharon Leder) of *Truth and Lamentation: Stories and Poems on the Holocaust*, nominated for the National Jewish Book Award. His story *Wising up* will be included in his short story collection, *A Teacher of the Holocaust and Other Stories*, to be published by Page Publishing in 2014. His painting and sculpture can be seen on www.teichmangallery.com

"As long as you can admire and love, then one is young forever."
Pablo Casals

ULTIMATE HAPPINESS

Peter Mellen

*S*urely *there must be something more to life than this?* I was miserable.

Throughout my adult life I've been fortunate enough to live a rich and unusual life, finding success in the world as a documentary filmmaker, best-selling author, and nationally known art history professor. And I've been through difficult life challenges—from being diagnosed with cancer, not once, but four times, to financial crises, hurricanes and floods. I wouldn't have missed any of it. My first wife Fran died from breast cancer; my second wife Linda struggled with chronic illness for fifteen years and died in 2010. I'm also someone who loves life passionately, and believes that good food, good wine, and good sex are just as "spiritual" as a path of renunciation and asceticism.

In my thirties I had everything most people dream of – family friends, fame, fortune. I recklessly sought out every pleasure I could find, but it still wasn't enough. In no time my marriage was in trouble and I was miserable. *What had I overlooked?* I asked myself. Then I noticed something was drawing me inward, and I had no idea what it was.

Then I stumbled into a yoga class and found a peace I had never known. Like a modern-day Don Quixote, I set out on a quest for spiritual enlightenment, which I imagined to be a state of unending bliss and joy. Before I knew it, I was standing on my head, meditating twice a day, purifying my body, improving myself, and healing myself. I was told that if I practiced, then practiced some more, that someday (or some future lifetime) I'd have this orgasmic mystical experience and be in permanent bliss.

Twenty years later I was no closer to my goal than when I began.

I wondered, What if all the traditional paths to enlightenment have got it all wrong? Surely there must be a direct path to self-realization? And, surely there must be a way of finding lasting happiness without having to give up the pleasures of sex, wine and chocolate!

It was then that I was introduced to the teachings of the great Indian sage Ramana Maharshi. I travelled the world to be with other teachers—Eckhart Tolle, Byron Katie, Gangaji, Adyashanti, and many others. They all shared a similar message: true happiness is not found somewhere off in the future. It is right here, right now as present-moment awareness. It is your natural state! What I had been looking for all these years had been there all along!

Linda and I wake up to sunshine and quiet. The palm trees are rustling in the wind outside the window. The Florida air is warm and moist. A small tugboat is making its way up the coastal waterway. Less than twenty-four hours ago we were back in Virginia in snow and ice. Did we somehow recreate the molecules that constitute a new reality overnight? If everything is an emanation of the mind, perhaps I'm really somewhere else and am projecting this whole scene with my mind?

I've signed up for a weeklong retreat with Francis Lucille, a French-born spiritual teacher. But why? I've attended so many retreats over the past few years. How many more do I have to go to before I get it? Who knows? Maybe this will be the last. The retreat is being held in a large rectangular room with floor to ceiling glass windows overlooking the Gulf of Mexico. Participants are chatting in small groups. Most of them seem to know each other. Francis is busy setting up his own sound system with the help of his wife Laura. Unlike most teachers, he doesn't have a whole crew of volunteers doing his work for him. I find a place by the windows and sit quietly with my eyes closed. My mind calms down. I'm relieved that I don't need to chat or make conversation.

I open my eyes and see Francis unceremoniously take his place at the front of the room and sit cross-legged on the floor. No dramatic entry with devotees holding doors open for him, no flowers around him, no pictures, no books—just a glass of water by his side. It's all very Zen. Francis is a slim, handsome dark-haired man in his forties, clean cut and healthy. There is a simple elegance about him that carries over into the way he dresses—a white polo shirt and khaki trousers.

He begins talking in his distinctive French accent. "When you make enlightenment an object," he says, "you will never find it. You are placing it off in the future somewhere, when it is right here."

Born in France, Francis was a pilot in the French Air Force, then a physicist and a diplomat for the French Government. I'm amused to think that he was a student in Paris at the same time I was. After a profound spiritual awakening in the 1970's, he gave up his career and moved to Middletown, California. He has been teaching all over Europe and the US for the last ten years.

"Your thoughts are not real," he says. "Your feelings are not real. All you need to do is accept the possibility that you are not a 'thing.' The truth is completely impersonal."

There is a long pause. He seems to search in some far off place for the right words. "The mind has to understand that enlightenment is totally beyond its reach. When this is understood, the mind becomes naturally quiet, because it has no place to go. This spontaneous and effortless stillness of the mind is pure welcoming. In this openness lies the opportunity to be knowingly that which we are."

I look around at the other participants. They are focused on him with rapt attention. I can tell by the blank expressions on some of their faces that they are hearing Francis for the first time. Francis is cerebral, and not for everyone. Others have been attending these same retreats for years. They nod knowingly as Francis talks. *How often do they need to hear these words before they get it? A hundred times—a thousand?* Then a light goes on. *They don't want to get it! They want this search to go on forever. They'll be hearing these same words years from now, and still nodding.*

Someone raises their hand and asks, "Does life have any purpose?"

There is a peal of laughter as the veteran retreat-goers turn to look at each other, as if to say, "Such a naïve question—do you remember when we used to ask questions like that?" Francis is unfazed. He ignores the tittering and he honors the questioner with total respect.

"Real life has no purpose," he says in his deliberate, slow manner of speaking. "Real life is pure joy, pure freedom. Now, if by life you mean this existence between birth and death, it could be said that its purpose is to know the truth."

As I sit there, it suddenly occurs to me that I don't need to hear this anymore. Maybe I've heard it for the hundredth time, maybe the thousandth. Maybe I'm bored with it all—whatever. It doesn't matter, I realize. I'm done. FINITO. FINISHED. It's time to say ENOUGH! The answer is not going to be found in this retreat or the next one. It won't come when the next teacher looks into my eyes and gives me a hit of shakti. It won't come when the next teacher says, "Peter, you're finally enlightened, you have my blessing—now go out and teach." Nor will it come when I do all kinds of austerities and spiritual practices that supposedly will bring me to awakening. These are just other ways of putting off what is right here, right now.

After the session I share this new understanding with Linda as we walk along the boardwalk back to our condo.

"I'm finally ready to call off the search," I say, squinting in the bright sunlight. "I'm finished with retreats." My bare feet are deliciously warm from walking on the sun-heated wooden planks of the boardwalk. I glance over at the wide stretch of beach and the Gulf of Mexico beyond. The wind is whipping the water into whitecaps and it looks muddy brown. A huge dredging machine pounds in pilings offshore: CLUNK, CLUNK, CLUNK.

"Well, at least you can be in the retreat," Linda says. "I can't even go into the room because of that toxic paint! But I'm just as happy to have my own retreat, watching the lizards and the birds."

"I like Francis. He doesn't seem to have any of the usual stuff around money, sex, or power." Over the years Linda and I have developed fine levels of distinction about spiritual teachers. Anything slightly off key leaps out like a flashing red light.

"I was thinking the same thing," says Linda. "He lives what he teaches. But what bothers me is that he talks about how we'll have perfect health and a transparent body if we let go of the body-mind identification. He promises that we'll all go to happy la-la land if we awaken. Ramana Maharshi would never say that. Bodies get sick and die. That's what they're supposed to do."

I let out a big sigh. "I'm *finally* getting that there's no such thing as the perfect teacher who has all the answers."

"They're all human, sometimes more human than we'd like."

"I've learned something from each one, but *they* can't do it for me."

"Only I can."

The boardwalk rises up over a dry creek bed, forming a small bridge. On either side there are low sand dunes covered with shrubs.

I'm so much in my head that I forgot where I am! Suddenly I start to notice all the life, all the smells, all the beauty that is around me. "Mmmm . . . Take a deep breath — salt air!"

Linda smiles and closes her eyes, breathing in. We lean on the railing, silent for a few moments. In that silence the world comes alive—butterflies struggling in the wind, seagulls flying overhead, the sand shifting at our feet, a vole darting through the underbrush.

"All this has been here all along," Linda says softly. "We just couldn't see it."

"*This* is why I came here," I say, putting my arm around her and looking into her eyes. "For this . . . *This!* The love is everywhere."

We hold each other tight, merging our bodies together. I nestle my face in her sun-drenched hair, smelling its sweet scent, the scent of the ocean, of life itself.

The sense of presence is so close that I can reach out and touch it. *This is the Beloved—a vast impersonal awareness. There is only the Beloved seeing the Beloved. My seeing is all "seeing"; I AM that seeing. My hearing is all "hearing"; I AM that hearing. It is effortless. It is ever-present. It is who I am. I don't have to go anywhere, do anything, or be with anyone to realize this. It's right here, right now.*

Where is there to go after this taste?

I stick it out to the end of the retreat, but I can't get into all the camaraderie of being with other seekers who are on "the search" together. It's time to go home to Virginia and just be quiet. The words of an old Chinese proverb came to mind: "Teachers open the door, but you must enter yourself."

When I see I am nothing that is wisdom and when I see that I am everything that is love. And between those two my life moves.
Nisargadatta

Peter Mellen is the author of *Ultimate Happiness: Chasing It, Finding It, Living It*, an entertaining memoir of his quest for ultimate peace and happiness. He has written three other books, including one that was a best-seller in Canada and another that was Book of the Year in 1979. He now lives in Maui.

HIS MILESTONE

Michael Levy

He worked hard, for Twenty-five years,
His business was a huge success,
The biggest in town,
A new milestone,
Hitting the headlines, in all the local newspapers,
Quite an achievement, since he started out with nothing,
He made a speech, saying he would retire soon,
Low and behold, new, more venturesome firms abounded,
Competition grew fierce,
No problem; he was up to the task,
After fifty years in the business, he was the biggest in the country,
A new milestone,
Catching the headlines, in all the national newspapers,
He gave a speech,
Saying he would definitely retire, very shortly,
However new, novel, unfamiliar competition snowballed,
Nevertheless, he was up to the task,
After sixty-five years in business, he was the biggest in the world,
A new milestone,

Striking the headlines, in every newspaper in the world,
That day as he prepared to make his speech to retire…
His milestone, became his headstone.

Michael Levy, world leader on the philosophy of truth and wisdom, is an international radio host, a mystical poet, business and finance philosopher and wellness/healthy living speaker on cruise ships, radio, TV and seminars. The Royal College of Psychiatry has published selected essays and poetry. Levy's works can be found on numerous websites.

"How old would you be if you didn't know how old you are?"
Satchel Paige

NO MAN IS AN ISLAND

Carmen Anthony Fiore

After we grow out of childhood, we think we are all grown up. Yeah, right. But we soon learn that we are just beginning our real education, which is dealing with earning a living, raising our families, and making decisions that will have a lifelong effect. Our schoolteachers never dealt with the "nitty-gritty" of life in our cocooned classrooms. And these days it seems as if they are more interested in boosting student self-esteem and passing the standardized one-size-fits-all federal proficiency test to get their school system needed federal money. It's all theory, no reality: reading, writing and arithmetic and maybe some history and geography and with a little civics thrown in for good measure. But this just doesn't cut it later when we need our adult thinking caps for those life-altering decisions, decisions, decisions.

They pile up on us like a mound of boulders on our chests. We can hardly breathe from the stress of them. But we forge on, thinking we're in control while remaining just as naïve as when we graduated from high school and college while waiting for our self-educating degree from the school of "hard knocks."

Ironically, I taught in a public school situation myself, after I got out of the military and eventually left a federal - and state-sponsored social-welfare program.

When I relocated my family in the 1970s from our comfortable suburban home located a few miles southeast of Trenton, New Jersey, to the "idyllic" woodlands of Hunterdon County some 25 miles north of Trenton, I was convinced I was doing the right thing: building a larger house on five acres of scenic woods next to a "harmless" shallow trout stream rippling over a bed of rocks.

We are talking sylvan heaven.

The Delaware Township officials requested I sign a waiver releasing them from any responsibility if the property floods by the adjacent creek. Our five-acre tract was on its expansive flood plain. The old light bulb must have blinked on above my head, but I never looked up, like a dummy, to notice its glaring brightness that was trying to tell me something.

Lulled by my arrogance, I thought nothing bad was ever going to happen to me or to my family up there, not while I was in charge, or should I say in control? Yeah, right. So, I signed the waiver (what a jerk!), then moved on to my "brave new world," (to quote Shakespeare's character, Miranda, in *The Tempest*) finally getting our dream house built next to a picturesque stream surrounded by tall cedar, oak and maple trees. I felt like an American pioneer of yesteryear, a modern-day Daniel Boone.

'Hey, nothing was going to stop me from attaining my goal of secluded, independent residential privacy,' I thought, 'and I'm still a privacy "nut," but that is another story with its own origin, theme and irony.'

A "What—me worry?" attitude became my mantra. "I don't sweat the small things in life," I say aloud to anybody who would listen to my overconfident musings.

My wife tried to warn me. She is not only smarter than I am, she is more savvy with a ton more common sense. She is the feet-on-the-ground realist; I'm the ephemeral, dreamy optimist. She was wary of the low-lying ground I had chosen to build on. She preferred the higher five-acre lots that were still available in the development tract, which were also farther from the creek. But not Mr. Sure-of-himself, yours truly. I insisted the cedar trees near the water were a special, even prettier asset that added to the scenery down there.

After my wife and I moved into our four-bedroom split-level with our two children and our pet mutt, Friskie, one of our friends visited us and suggested we start building a four-foot-high crescent-shaped berm facing the creek side. 'It was an astute suggestion, since the water was only about 75 feet from our dwelling,' I thought derisively.

I sloughed off the idea. What did he know? Besides, it sounded like too much work and trouble, piling dirt, tree trunks and rocks for a distance of about 400 feet to be effective. And where would I get all that dirt and rock? I was not going to pay somebody to truck it in. I had emptied our bank account to buy the land and to make the required down payment in order to get the construction started. (But that was another dumb move, not leaving a cash reserve in the bank account for contingencies.) Besides, it would have looked unnatural. God forbid!

How long did it take to have my dream turn into a nightmare?

Less than a year, when back-to-back hurricanes swept in from the Atlantic Ocean across New Jersey during August, 1971. They saturated the ground and swelled the streams and rivers that rose over their banks, inundating the adjacent fields. All the low-lying properties got drowned. And our supposedly harmless narrow creek became a torrent of overflowing white water. Its spreading menace engulfed every square inch of ground around our house.

To make things worse, it happened at night, which really irritated me. I felt helpless. I had to wait for daylight to fight back against Mother Nature, the bitch! We didn't have time to get the cars to higher ground. We did manage to lug our furniture out of the den up to the living room. I had to wade through the rising water in our basement to shut off the electric power switches, then get back to the stairs before the chilling water rose to eye level—and without getting myself electrocuted.

Thankfully, the water came in fast, rose to about a foot-plus in our den, the adjacent built-in two-car garage, the lavatory and the laundry room after filling the basement, then left our house completely a few hours later. Thank God it didn't linger for days like some bigger, wider river floods do. Although it was short-lived, the physical damage was longer-lasting, all the while the subtle psychological effects became embedded in our psyches—to surface later in seemingly spontaneous marital disagreements.

I didn't say it out loud, but I had to admit to myself that I should have listened to my wife and to our friend's berm-building suggestion. I could have kicked my own bony rear end for being such a stubborn idiot.

What did I learn from our personal catastrophe?

We are not in charge on this planet. My self-confidence took a beating that night and again the following day when surveying the damage from a better vantage point. It was a humbling experience going head-to-head against the unseen forces of nature like the howling wind and the relentless driving rain, toppling trees and knocking them over like a bowling alley's ten pins.

Later, the negative results morphed into a positive lesson for me.

I witnessed firsthand that people have a good side, and it reveals itself in times of tragedy and suffering. Our neighbors came to our rescue. They helped us clean and restore the washer and the dryer, and to get our cars back to working condition again, draining the water out of the engines, as well as drying out the oil-fired furnace and the basement, which also needed its cinder-block walls hosed down thoroughly, cleaning off the muck left by the receding water. They helped us do all that tedious work without our asking them to; it was touching. I'll never forget their unconditional generosity; the giving of their time and effort on our behalf. And they never once said, I told you so.

Another lesson learned brought to mind the old adage: "No man is an island." I became more appreciative and accepting of others and their opinions as I aged, finally realizing how much we need one another on this earth to simply survive. And I can trace that personal growth in me back to that devastating flood of our new home up in 'God's country.'

Hey, maybe a little induced humility is good for us. I know it was good for me in the long run. I even started to listen to my wife's advice after that.

As a social worker and a school teacher, C.A. Fiore wrote part time. Now he writes full time: fiction, novels, short stories, nonfiction self-help books, essays and articles, and screenplays (12 listed with Amazon Studios). He has 34 books listed for downloading from Amazon's Kindle bookstore. His website: www.carmenanthonyfiore.com

"If I can stop one Heart from breaking
I shall not live in vain
If I can ease one Life the Aching'
Or cool one in Pain
Or help one fainting Robin
Unto his Nest again
I shall not live in Vain."

Emily Dickenson

EVERYDAY ALCHEMY

Jewell Reinhart Coburn

"Man, what a drag. Are we looking at one more lost weekend?"

Against all my hopes, here he is beginning his usual tirade and he hasn't even gotten himself and his bags all the way through the front door.

It had been my wish, one born out of desperation, that I could re-engineer things from the start, move into a new place, establish a whole different and better atmosphere around here. A little family harmony, that's all I'm looking for. But, no, once again, it looks like I've failed. My son, my first born, now a college Junior has said barely a dozen words upon returning from his semester away – and off we go. Once again those same old feelings of maternal anguish I've tried to stuff down so many times before are right here again and crawling up my spine.

Vince is relentless. "I'm put off and I'm disturbed right to my DNA," he's saying. "No matter what I do, nothing, Mom, nothing gets me the ear that your druggy baby boy gets in this family. For crying out loud, I need to feel some support. You pushed me into the honors program. It's incredibly demanding, and I need to know you're with me."

"Is this because I couldn't make it to your Honors ceremony, Dear? But I thought I explained . . ."

Of course I could try to counter Vince's complaints and accusations, but what good will it do? Extraordinary as it is, this young man is disgruntled and out-of-sorts at what he has for so long perceived to be his un-esteemed place within the family. And all of this – outrageously – in the very face of easy entitlements: We're looking at the young Vincent Stanley Hartford, V., about to enter the long line of esteemed scientists in the family, an assured legacy. But regardless, there persists in him what seems like an emotional black hole that stubbornly refuses to be filled – and it looks as though I fit into this equation, but I'm just not sure how.

"So, I have to go it alone," he murmurs, resolve tinged with a forlorn resignation. "So what else is new?" He reaches, without needing sight, deep into the refrigerator's interior for comfort food probably in the form of ham and cheese on sourdough.

"Now, Vince," I hear myself begin my usual, and by now, worn out response, "You know we're proud of you. We couldn't be more pleased with your accomplishments. Your grades certainly please us and should certainly satisfy you as well."

"You say that now," he goes on, and suddenly I feel myself tensing, knowing already what I'm in for. "But perhaps your word, 'pleased' would be better exchanged with the word, 'expected.' Like really, Mom, why did you have to miss my Honors assembly? It's not that long a drive to the campus. We both know that. So you had a little last minute emergency. So you always have little last minute emergencies. This time, you probably had to tend to one more Cop's summons. Talk about 'old news.' Baby brother Davy, caught red-handed again, no doubt. No, don't bother. You don't have to tell me. I've been down that road too many times already."

Just then, thankfully, the phone rings. I turn to pick it up. Vince, not about to compete with anyone, and certainly not with a voice on the phone line, goes on down the hall to his room, lugging along his bulging laundry bag and pushing his suitcase ahead of him.

Just then, Sara, Vince's sister, breezes into the kitchen, slipping out of her backpack. "Hold it, Mom. Don't take that call. Hang up. Tell 'em you'll call them back. You and I gotta talk because Jill's at it again. What's the matter with that other daughter of yours? She's gotta stop rifling through my things. You gotta talk to her, Mom. This has got to stop!"

I'm mute. I'm standing here holding the phone, and suddenly I'm thinking how red-faced I'd be if this scene taking place in my kitchen with two of my four teenagers, were being recorded for a Dr. Phil TV show.

Sara pushes on: "We all know what Jill's hunting for. She's probably in my things hunting for one more of my papers, probably one you insisted I re-write to *your* specifications, Mom – only to have my teacher tell me I hadn't followed *her* directions. Mom, you gotta stop this, you're not a teacher anymore. You've been away from the classroom plenty long by now, and you're out of step. What you have to do is stop her. That's all. Make Jill shape up. Don't you have any idea that what you're doing is wrong?"

I catch the sound of the dial tone. Obviously, and thankfully, I missed the call. I can only trust my overworked angels to shield the poor caller from hearing this troublesome domestic harangue.

"That's not all, Mom . . . ," Sara can't seem to stop herself when with that, her sister Jill bursts into the kitchen, their words firing like bullets in savage crossfire.

"You gotta stay away from my friends, Mom," Jill warns loudly, her voice overpowering her sister's. Breathlessly she snatches up the moment and slices her way through to me too. "Mom," she shouts accusingly, "You don't tell my friends what my schedule is. Ever! That's my business. You don't tell my friends what I can and can't do."

"Jill, back off," Sarah assumes the adult version of her fifteen year-old self. "I was talking to Mom first. You're interrupting."

"Now Jill, and Sarah – both of you – you know I wouldn't intentionally do a thing like that."

"Well, maybe not intentionally, Mom, but you did it all the same. And that's just plain wrong."

Jill is on a roll now, fueled by her own sense of rightness and indignation. I've been through this so many times I know exactly how fast it can escalate. Is there no way to short-circuit this mania, I wonder one more time? Why do I feel so helpless to bring peace to this house?

"Please understand, Dears," I say, leaning against the kitchen counter and holding up my hands for quiet, "Whatever I do, I'm only trying to help. This is a busy few days for all of us – trying to pull together this family event – making reservations for everyone coming from so far away, wanting things to be comfortable for Uncle Carl so soon out of surgery, and for Grandmother Riley with her leg problems."

I take note that my feeble attempts to bring sanity obviously fail to defuse the moment. Innocently, or so I thought at the time, I had told Jill's friend about the upcoming family gathering, the one Vince made a special effort to return from college to attend, the one Jill, along with the rest of the family would be expected to help out with. And yes, I was sorry for the confusion of dates, but what is, is. Don't families usually work things out?

"Besides all this," Jill speaks up indignantly, "Where's Davy? Why isn't he here? We all agreed to get home early from school today to help. We're here. Even Vince is back from college. So, where's Davy? I sure hope what I'm hearing at school isn't true. The rumor is he's going camping with his buddies this weekend. How did he get a reprieve?"

Suddenly I can hardly draw a breath, so much oxygen has been sucked from the room.

Jill persists. "It's probably his marijuana thing again. He can't stay away from it. That stuff sure attracts him more than this family shindig. Come on, let's face it, that kid's known about these plans the same as the rest of us. Look, Mom, I really resent this."

Suddenly Vince rejoins the fray: "Let me make it known that I am personally fed up with bailing out that little brother of mine when you and Dad are off at some conference. I'm done with fronting for him."

Can this be believed? I think to myself. My young people haven't been all together as a family for months, and yet there are no hellos. No warm greetings. No engaging smiles. Not a hug or a handshake – just the usual backbiting. It's gone way beyond toxic. We're edging toward *lethal*.

"Hand over my paper, Jill." Sara turns accusingly to her younger sister who is already picking through the bowl of fruit on the kitchen counter. "I know you took it."

Under her breath, Jill mutters, "You lie."

"Mom, you hear that? Jill's calling me a liar. She's telling me she didn't take my paper when anybody can see she's been in my things. Isn't there something about 'Thou shalt not lie,' some place? How about, 'Thou shalt not steal.' Or, let's try another one, how about not bearing false witness? Well, Mom, you heard her. Do something!"

"Yeah, Mom," Jill parrots her sister. "Do something, and Jill looks me square in the eyes, defiantly. "If you hadn't been so generous with your theme writing skills, Mom, maybe we'd all be more respectful of each other's work. The way it is now, everyone just figures if they wait long enough, you'll do it for them. Gotta tough essay assignment? Not to worry. If ya want it fast, just go to the heap of stuff Mom's already written. Easy."

"Come on, Mom, your own mother was a teacher." I feel all six eyes turned my way. "Is that what Gram did for you? Did she do your homework? Well, heck, if Mom has to save her own face so much by having us all be the big super-achieving kids she likes to boast about, well, so she ends up doing our work for us. Who are we to complain?" Jill rolls her eyes and pops another grape into her mouth.

"But still, it's not for you to go into my room, Jill, and go through *my* things, no matter *who* wrote the paper."

Suddenly I feel I'm in a Jackson Pollack world, flayed out against a massive canvas, splashed with primary colors to the background music of the most cacophonous Stravinsky score. How, I am asking myself, did life with these young people come to this? They've successfully played the blame game, the self-entitlement game; they've become master abusers, and blind to anything beyond their own immediate interests. And I've been swept up into their vitriol. Competition trumps cooperation in this bull-pen of a household. They've thoroughly demonstrated that for whatever reason lies beneath it all, not one of them can be held in any way responsible for anything they do or not do. Is this our era's take on 'the devil made us do it?"

"Yeah, Mom," Vince, at it again, "ya oughta listen. She does have a point, you know."

Clearly, I've contributed to this. But how? And how can this cauldron, boiling over with ill feelings, disrespect for others, absence of familial warmth, lack of civility, awash in adolescent hormones be cooled and metamorphosed into the kind of family I want so badly. What this has come to will take alchemy far beyond my skills to conjure.

Just then, Sara speaks up, "By the way, Mom, we'll no sooner get through this family affair than we'll be faced with Christmas. Christmas means gifts and gifts mean money. You know what you always say about honoring our mother and father. And in this family's case, that means the grandparents too. I guess we better plan ahead for that now too."

And off we go again.

Yeah," Vince adds, and how am I supposed to earn money when I'm in college and carrying all these extra units? How can I hold down an outside job?"

"Me too," whines Jill. "How will I have anything left for presents after I've spent everything I have on what I need for the winter prom when all my formals are summer ones?"

"And, if I don't get paid," adds Sara, "I won't have enough money to make even a paper-clip necklace for you, Mom, like I did back in pre-school. You think Dad will go for a chunk of painted rock for a Christmas paperweight again?"

Suddenly, through the blazing mass of chaotic adolescent energies, there comes a single, pure ray of insight. Where it comes from, I haven't the slightest idea, but one thing I sense is that I must lose no time in scooping it up and tucking it firmly into my mind, urged on by a knowing beyond my understanding that this is meant for the precise moment that will be exactly right.

⁓

The sharp autumn winds yield to the first gentle snow fall. House by house, colored lights go up. It's a festive time and with it comes the expected questions from the young people about exactly what I, as Mother, want for Christmas. Urged by a sense of tradition, they begin their plans to "honor thy father and thy mother," not with respect and kind words, sadly, but rather with some kind of tangible, probably showy gift. Vince phones from college to ask. Sara comes into my office, sits down by my desk, and asks. Jill, over oatmeal one morning, asks. And David, by a post-it stuck directly to the center of my computer screen, asks. Each of my four young people has been careful to remind me yet again that they are nearing the point of exhausting their meager savings earned from our family program of earned-allowances along with the few outside jobs they have been able to get.

To each, individually, I respond that I'll get back to them and I thank them for asking. Then I devise my plan.

I take from that place deep in my mind, where I'd so intentionally placed it, that flash of insight, that wisp of wisdom that had made its way through the family chaos that afternoon back in the kitchen. And I make the determined decision to talk personally with each of the young people – separately, individually.

To each, I hear myself saying a version of the following:

"First off, Dear, I want to tell you how much I appreciate you. I do love you so much and I'm proud and thankful you are my child. It is kind of you that you want to give me a well-selected gift this year, and that you want it to be something that I especially want, or especially need. I respect that you are on a tight budget, and that your work and study-loads are heavy. I honor that. None-the-less, because you ask, I will give you my answer. Yes, there really is something I very much want from you this year, and Christmas is a very good time for it to be given, though any time can be just as perfect.

At this, I can hear each of them inhaling, momentarily holding their breath, and most likely thinking, "Oh brother, what's she going to lay on me this time?"

I give no time for interruption. I go on, speaking to each in our own carefully carved out one-on-one time. "What I very much want is something that's really easy to obtain, and very easy to give. It has no weight to it. It requires no shopping time. And, best of all, it will cost you nothing."

At this, I hear a huge, expired breath – one of obvious relief on the part of each young person. And in response, each is probably asking in their own way, "OK, is this some kind of silly trick?"

In anticipation of their reaction, I add, "This is no trick. It is not a joke."

"Well then. . .?"

"What I want from you is nothing more or less than the gift of your forgiveness."

To that, I am confronted with silence, their expression, one of confusion.

"Don't answer right now," I go on. "There's no need to. Just allow yourself to mull it over. Perhaps think about why I might ask for a gift like this. Think a bit about times and words and events when to forgive could have nipped noisy conflict right off at its root. Then take a hold of that moment. Wrap it up in your mind. Ribbon it with your most heartfelt intentions – and by the way, think about putting enough forgiveness in that package that it can spill over to your brothers and sisters too.

Then think of your grandparents. After all, consider the possibility of their shortcomings where their upbringing of their daughter, me, your mother, is concerned. I have had to forgive my own parents in my own way. Then see where those traits filtered through to impact you. I think it's safe to say you will find this gift one of the most important you'll ever give this entire lifetime."

In the silence that follows, each of the four young people seems momentarily alone with their thoughts, and then, "You mean you really want nothing, nothing but *this* for Christmas? No gift we can put under the tree?"

"That's right, Dear. Nothing. Nothing at all because in this case, this Nothing, as you call it, becomes Everything.

And so, as it has turned out through the years, there has been no need to remind them about what they consented to. In difficult moments, even though all are now adults with their own children, we from time to time give each other *the look*, accompanied by a touch of silence, just enough to let the amazing dynamic of forgiveness work its magic.

TURKEY

Andrew Merton

A wild turkey appears in my yard,
a fine fellow with a fiery red wattle.
Under the oak he spreads his tail feathers,
struts, looks around,
and wanders off.
He displays himself three more times,
then disappears. As will I.
And then what will you say of me,
all of you, wife, children,
colleagues, students, friends?
He was a fine fellow.
Such a shame he was never fine enough
to suit himself.
A few decades left, at most.
Time to stop preening.

My book, *Evidence that We Are Decended from Chairs*, was published by Accents Publishing in 2012. My work has appeared in the *Bellevue Literary Review, Alaska Quarterly Review, The Realto* (U.K.), *The Comstock Review, The American Journal of Nursing*, and elsewhere. I teach writing at the University of New Hampshire.

'DYING' IN THE PULPIT

Joe Novara

There aren't too many times I've laughed out loud during a sermon. But I've always thought it was the perfect place to drop a straight line — a comic's dream: a captive audience, dead serious material and then the chance to catch the crowd off guard. Irresistible. I can't say I was looking for a chance to get a rise out of my congregation but the possibility was always there.

There was a time in my life, in my late twenties, when I served in a Detroit parish as a Roman Catholic priest. There was much that I learned from that time of ministry which carried on into my later years.

One Sunday, late March, snow melting, winter loosening its grip, I was in the middle of my tight, ten minute sermon that I had worked on for ten hours the preceding week. I always worked hard on the word—trying to reach people's minds. I wanted to share whatever I could of what I had learned in my theological studies in Rome from some of the top scholars in their fields.

One of my key topics came from my moral theology professor, Father Fuchs—a cross between Cary Grant and a U-Boat commander. He made a lasting impression on me by propounding his favorite theme: St. Paul ... Liberty ... and the Law. His approach, based on the Pauline epistles, recommended getting past the letter of the law and enjoying the freedom of Christian love. His message: "Get your mind straight about right and wrong and follow it ... internalize the moral imperatives of religion and get beyond the pharisaical tediousness of minute laws" stood in marked contrast to another professor, Father Maurizio Zalba who exemplified Jesuit nit-picking casuistry in the extreme.

I, of course, had dutifully purchased Zalba's 1,500, onion-skin paper tome of case upon case of moral predicaments he proposed to resolve. One in particular stood out. The problem described was: What if a young man, while riding his motorcycle to work got sexually aroused and ejaculated? Was it a sin and could he continue to ride? Zalba's answer was: He could ride his cycle on the way to work on weekdays but he could not indulge in pleasure riding on the weekends.

Shortly after that course, I converted that manual-for-righteous-living to a doorstop and welcomed the more intelligent approach of Father Fuchs and his interpretation of St. Paul.

I took my sermons seriously and refused to simply mouth feel-good platitudes. The longer I was in the parish the more my message focused on the challenge of self-realization, to think through the rules of the church, and come to personal acceptance or rejection of them. For example, even if birth control was prohibited by the church, each adult still had to make a mature, responsible decision for his or her family. I couldn't come out in favor of birth control from the pulpit, but I could encourage my congregation in general terms to take charge of their own moral decisions and to have the courage of their convictions. But more and more I was trying to tell folks to think on their own, to move past reliance on the church for every moral decision in their lives.

The primacy of individual consciousness and the possibility of growing past a need for mother church was not exactly a message compatible with long-time job security. But that was the only true message I felt like I could advance at the time.

So, there I was, that winter Sunday, preaching on my chosen theme ... St. Paul, Liberty, and the Law when suddenly a huge chunk of melting ice rumbled down the three story high slate roof of the church. I stopped for the expectant pause as we all waited for the thundering crash in the courtyard on the other side of the stained glass windows.

This was my chance for an improv straight line. In the hushed pause, I tilted my head toward the rafters and said, "If you're inclined to disagree with that last statement, I could always rephrase..." I looked back down to a sea of blank, uncomprehending faces. Not a flicker of connection. Nada. Then the crash of fallen snow and, with it, my moment of clarity ... I was on a different page from my congregation. I was preaching to a blank wall. I could have simply repeated the Lord's Prayer over and over and they would have been just as satisfied with my sermon. The retired priest in our rectory could have mouthed bromides and they would have been happy ... happier probably. It wasn't even that they didn't see the humor in the situation —or that they were a 'tough crowd' as Don Rickles would say. I was wasting my energy in a self-defeating effort for people who only wanted to be reassured, not challenged to confront their beliefs.

As I stood at the pulpit, I could acknowledge that some changes had occurred since the conclusion of the Vatican Council three years earlier. A communion rail no longer separated the faithful from the sanctuary. The altar behind me now faced the congregation. I said mass in English. The faithful sang new hymns. But, as I 'died' there that Sunday morning, I was confronted with the fact that the majority of my congregation wasn't buying what I was selling. They weren't even in the market. They could endure the jarring superficial changes being imposed on them, but deep down, I believe, they yearned for the way their religion used to be.

So what did I learn not to do from this experience? I learned not to bang my head against a wall. It's not enough to be sincere, to want to care for others. I learned that it's possible to be the right person in the wrong place and it does no good to force myself to fit in.

I also learned, and which has served me well into my senior years, not to try to spend a lot of time or energy trying to change an institution and the people in it from the inside. Others may think differently but for me, the result was self-defeating. Oh yes, I learned too that as a matter of practice, it's best to eschew improvisational pulpit humor.

A retired trainer and college writing instructor, Joe Novara lives in Kalamazoo, Michigan, where he regularly adds to his ePublished backlist of books, stories and poems. https://www.smashwords.com/profile/view/Joenovara and a blog on writing for homeschooled boys http://joenovara.wordpress.com

A MOVING EXPERIENCE

Judy Warner Scher

For the past few years, I have escaped from the Virginia winters by going away for two months. After my husband died in June 2003, I chose to visit close friends who live in warm places like Florida or Hawaii. But this past January I decided I didn't need that personal safety net anymore so I flew to Santa Barbara, a place I had passed through briefly. Online, I discovered a vacation rental in nearby Summerland. Friends gave me names of people to contact. I loved the weather, the beauty of the Spanish architecture, views unimpeded by billboards, the wide white beaches and the salty ocean air. Everyone I met was friendly and helpful and I felt totally at home in this charming seaside town.

When I returned home to Charlottesville, where I had close friends, a wonderful dance community, work, good medical care and a beautiful house on a lake, I felt my time there had completed its course. For 18 years, I had been happy in Virginia but my heart told me to move to California. I decided to put my house on the market to see what would happen. Meanwhile, my mind was screaming, "You're in your sixties! Are you crazy giving up such a comfortable and happy life?"

Unbelievable as it may seem given the 2009 housing market, I had a deal in 13 days. I sold my house and most of the furnishings to a young couple just starting out their lives together.

Over and over my friends would say to me, "You have so much courage. I can't believe at your age you could just pick up and move across the country on your own."

What they didn't understand is that it has nothing to do with courage. I was just following a strong inner prompting. When you do this, everything seems to flow.

Within a week of returning to Santa Barbara, I found the perfect place to rent in Montecito: a two bedroom, two bath apartment with a terrace and a distant view of the ocean. How freeing it is to just call downstairs and say the garbage disposal isn't working and the manager appears immediately to fix it. After 18 years of owning a home, what a treat!

A woman I met this past winter has been like my guardian angel, inviting me to join her at art openings, jazz clubs, checking in on me to see I was okay, introducing me to new people. I immediately started dancing, which is always a source of joy for me.

What is most amazing to me though is how open people are here. For instance, one day I met a woman at a café. She was planning to go to Argentina to study tango. We exchanged numbers and the next day she called and asked me, "Do you like jazz?"

"I love it."

"Tomorrow Nate Birkey is playing at Soho. Do you want to meet me?"

"Great!" It turned out to be a lovely lunch with good jazz

Another day, an attractive man in his 50's walking out of Vons said to me,

"Isn't it a beautiful day?"

"Yes, but every day is like this," I replied.

Upon hearing my accent he said, "Where are you from?"

"I just moved here three weeks ago from Charlottesville, but I'm originally from New York City."

"I'm from the East coast too. Tell me," he said with great intensity, "What do you think of the people out here?"

"I think they're great – much warmer than on the East coast. Everyone is so welcoming."

"Yes, but they're not as *deep*," he said stressing the word.

"Well, I've only been here a few weeks and am not into *deep* right now; I'm into furniture!"

After introducing ourselves, he said, "Would you like to have drinks at the Biltmore one evening?"

Surprised, but open to the idea, I said, "Sure."

Who knows if he'll call, but the point is just how open people are here.

There is definitely stress involved in adjusting to a new environment. Driving has been the most challenging. On the East coast, we look to see if there is a car coming before we get on a highway. Here you rev up to 60 miles an hour and, by the Grace of God, weave your way onto 101. I am better at it now, but for weeks I was terrified every time I had to get on the freeway.

Waking up every morning to beautiful weather is a real boon. No humidity and no more freezing winters to run away from. Instead, I take a short eight-minute stroll from my apartment to the beach where, surrounded by beauty, I can breathe in the crisp ocean air as I take my morning walk.

Everything is new: the sights, the smells, the people and, of course, my experiences. I feel alive and alert. This alone is a good enough reason to move. After saying this I realize it's not about choosing to move, it's about listening to your heart so that when it's your time, change just happens. We're told moving is one of the most stressful things in life along with divorce and death. But when your heart moves you, it can be a wonderful new adventure.

PART 3

When Life Hands You A Zinger

BLINDSIDED

Nancy Katz

I became liberated at 65. That's when I learned I'd been living on the "other side of the closet." How slow a learner am I? That slow. Slow enough to be unable to figure out that my marriage was knotty and unfulfilling, not because I wasn't the right kind of woman but because I *was* a woman, not a man. So for over forty-five years, I was his "beard."

Liberation came in the form of learning he was gay. It put everything in perspective. My gender was what was wrong with me, not my looks nor my brains nor my tastes nor my choices.

The honeymoon should have opened my eyes. It was one week of cold gloomy rain on Cape Cod with a dead whale washed up on the beach. He spent most of the days with hometown auto mechanic buddies. I spent my time being lonely. He was drunk throughout. I am not a drinker.

I can't even remember what I expected. We married in 1959. I was dazzled by how different he was from the crewneck sweater and chino boys from my hometown. His family was New York liberal intellectual. He was a rebel: ducktail haircut, cigarette pack rolled in his short-sleeved shirt, pegged pants and fast cars.

Adventure! Excitement! The only intellectual discussions in my family were arguments between my Eisenhower-Republican father and egalitarian me. So here was the excitingly different young man with a family that was enticing. I fell for the package. I knew so much at nineteen. Next to nothing is what I knew.

In retrospect I can see that much of the time he was trying to push me away so he wouldn't have to repress his sexuality. I was foolishly steadfast. All his antagonistic put-downs, all the physical rebuffs simply contributed to my feeling there had to be something wrong with me. I couldn't even take the hint when he'd apologize for not being able to meet my sexual needs and even suggesting he'd understand if I fooled around with someone else. Eventually I did have two short-lived affairs but, even though this was his idea, he reacted totally differently from the way I expected; he actually seemed hurt. In spite of my gender incorrectness, perhaps he did love me.

So after years and years of frustration and acute loneliness and trying to compensate by throwing myself into raising three children, I more or less dropped out and tuned out.

When I was forty-five we went into business with my riding trainer and her sociopath boyfriend. We had bought a horse farm with our money, and they were to provide the sweat equity. It was doomed to fail for so many reasons and it did. My husband was beside himself with the failure of our partners to do anything but absorb more and more of our cash.

In the end, the sociopath boyfriend was doing his best to turn me against my husband by telling me that he was gay and living a deceitful life, which I wouldn't believe. The sociopath was convinced that my husband had millions of dollars squirreled away, and he figured if he could steer me toward divorce, then I would get his millions, which would be available to support him and the love of his life, my trainer. I finally had enough and, with my husband, we resolved to sell the farm and get my horses out of there.

Later that same day I walked into our house. I saw my husband looking fragile and pained in a way I had never seen before. "What's wrong?" I asked.

Suddenly he burst out in tears. After years of hiding, he finally broke down and told me that the young man he had been in love with for the past three years was going to leave him. He then went on to tell me his lover had slept in our bed while I was out of town at horse shows. Suddenly, I could hardly breathe. Betrayal engulfed me. I felt viscerally revolted.

With that, the door swung wide open. It took hardly any time at all to know that this was my liberation.

Finally we decided to separate and keep it simple. I finally made up my mind to move out, to have a house of my own, and dog of my own.

I tried my hand at the Internet dating game. But at the age of sixty-five it was more than challenging. It was like middle school dances: boys lined up on one side of the gym and going for the Barbie dolls, one that I am not. After what seemed like many hilarious disasters, I took a chance on someone who was not an animal person, and he took a chance on me – an older woman.

How was the sex? It was thrilling. I had forgotten what it was like to be sexually desirable. It was mind boggling to be awakened in the dead of night by a man with a hard-on kissing the back of my neck. The fact that I was sixty-five didn't seem to make any difference. My customary 6:30 a.m. wake-up time moved to 11 a.m. It was a totally different world and aside from feeling a bit lost with half the day gone, I loved every minute of it.

In time, passion has moved on to warm and comfortable, but it was one hell of a rush while it lasted.

Man, dog, and I have been together since 2006. The house is ten acres from where my husband lives. The children are all fine now with the way things have worked out.

After so many years of an "unsatisfactory" relationship, it is affirming to know I can have a rewarding one – one based on mutual trust and communication. I am feeling capable and competent now and I'm not feeling lonely anymore. Being lonely in a relationship is the worst lonely of all.

I was raised in suburban New Jersey in the 40s and 50s followed by a marriage at nineteen. We raised three children in Connecticut. I became involved in local politics, teaching young children, horses, dogs, hiking the nearby woods and gardening. I've continued the outdoor activities and enjoy my family.

BLESSED

Diana M. Amadeo

My fifties came on like a bang with hot flashes, night sweats, mood swings and insomnia. Instead of meeting these midlife body changes with dread, silently I cheered. As a registered nurse I know that menopause is a normal, healthy milestone in a woman's life. Men and women both are confronted with mid-life changes – their own menopause. Yet the key word here is *normal*. For a dozen years or more my life had been far from normal. I felt like shouting to the world – "I'm making the change, I'm menopausal. I am discovering the crone within. Do you hear that? I am *normal*."

After a decade plus of canes, crutches, wheelchairs and motorized scooters, today I walk unaided. Constant abnormal physical changes from Multiple Sclerosis altered my vision, hearing and mobility. The neuropathy pain was sometimes excruciating. But now at this point in time, I am in remission and enjoying my body, spirit and mind, be it ever so humble and imperfect. Menopausal? No sweat. Living with MS has prepared me for constant physical change. The menopausal symptoms I have now just seem to flow with the natural progression of things.

The way I see it is that women are blessed with three stages of life – maiden, mother and crone.

Maidenhood found me one of ten children in a busy, not so nurturing household. Mother was exhausted and ultra-religious. Father was mostly absent. I often labeled my childhood as "loneliness in a crowd," with fierce competition to be seen or heard. When I grew up and stopped blaming childhood for my problems, I realized that my childhood was in fact, pretty good: playful, inquisitive, creative, educational and full of love, but a different type of love – a love of self-reliance, determination and imagination.

Motherhood for me was more difficult, keeping a long term marriage on track, raising three children and establishing two separate careers while dealing with a chronic debilitating illness. There were times I didn't feel I could go on. With a lot of luck, faith and family support I did survive. Through patience, and hard work, my thirty year marriage became strong, my children thrived and the entire family became more compassionate.

So now I am a crone, a fierce lioness who has survived life's struggles. What didn't kill me has left me stronger, yet with enough softness to nurture others in need. I am wiser simply from experiencing life up to now. I see my advancing age not as a burden but as a sacred gift. It saddens me that some of my friends have left this earth before experiencing what it is to become a crone.

To be a "crone" or a "wise woman" means to accept the divine nod in recognition of her inner strength. I have been tested with hardships and obstacles and have dug deep to overcome them. I didn't give up even when tempted. I faced my mistakes, took ownership, begged forgiveness and moved on. When I hit rock bottom I refused to sink into the mud of despair. I put on my shoes with springs of resiliency and bounced right back onto the playing field.

I have tapped into an empowerment that is uniquely my own. I am able to look over the rich, colorful tapestry of my life with a sense of pride and deep satisfaction. A job well done – but it's not a job that's over. If something is wrong, if an opportunity is missed, there is still time to make things right.

I see these as my creative years. I have seen many stories come full circle. Oftentimes, circumstance denies the opportunity to see, first hand, justice emerge from injustice. But nature seems to be constructed in a way that for every action there is a reaction. Finally I can let go of manipulation and cruelty to others much better now than in the past because of the many times life has shown me that ultimately what goes around does come around. Lies, political spin, attempts to use God to further a personal agenda - all become more transparent to the crone.

The crone has developed a maturity about letting go. Detaching is invigorating. Holding onto pain is draining. The crone has learned to set reasonable boundaries to honor her inner strength and peace. I have learned that personal success is the best revenge. I use my energy toward positive outcomes and don't allow my positive energy to be drained by those who decide to live destructively. Forgiveness is necessary; it need not condone another's bad behavior nor be immediate, but be allowed to evolve.

The years ahead will likely bring further health concerns, and certainly the empty nest syndrome, sandwich generational issues and loss of family and friends. But I, like the crone, have honed an outlook on life that lets me be patient and resourceful, and to deal with life gracefully. The crone that I am has survived, and now moves through the rest of her life with understated knowledge, having accumulated experience, and power, while at the same time being open to learn, even the simplest things.

She learns that wearing cotton is preferred over polyester or velour during hot flashes, that cotton or flannel sheets beat silk any day for night sweats. She learns to hold her tongue because of others' biting remarks. She learns to make peace with insomnia by taking a refreshing midday nap in the hope that insomnia's purpose is to watch a spectacular sunrise or to hear the heavenly rhythmic snore of a loving spouse.

I embrace my crone-hood. I love who I am right now at this stage in my life. Can it get any better than that?

Award winning author Diana M Amadeo has in excess of 500 publications which include books, ebooks, anthologies, magazines and newspapers. She has ten stories in various *Chicken Soup for the Soul* books. She lives in a wooded writer's hideaway in the Greater Boston area. Visit her at http://www.facebook.com/DianasWritings

INTO THE UNKNOWN

R. R. Hart

What a predicament. Who knows why I listened to them . . . or why I let myself be talked into taking the Precipice, the highest peak in the ski park. Now I'm left to watch my ski-buddies skimming the shivery snow, off and down the mountain and out of sight. Not one of them slowed their stunning descent. And here I am. Alone. A far too novice skier at this time in my life, and on a much too hostile terrain.

It's the last run of the day. The lifts are about to close. Already the mountain's hot-shot skiers have made their graceful high-speed exodus swinging out around me, churning huge sprays of snow in their wake. I'm leaning on my ski poles planted precariously into the steep slope. Did I really think I could keep up with the others? At sixty-seven? What was I thinking? And now, I know I'm in for it . . . big time.

I look around and suddenly the whole mountain has gone silent. There's an ominous quality to the solitude. A darkening chill settles in on the fast deserted slopes. Once the ski lift comes to a stop, the chairs will swing back and forth on their cables, then settle into an empty stillness. The way I see it is that I don't have many choices. I hadn't kept up my skiing skills over the years, and now I'm in a fix. I'm tired. Awfully tired. My muscles feel spongy, and my destination down mountain is fading into evening twilight.

But I've got to get off this mountain – and get off fast.

There's no way I can rely on the trusty snow plow we used as kids, forcing my ski tips together with the back runners splayed out in a wedge. That tactic's used for slowing to a gentle stop on easier inclines. And this incline is far too sheer a drop. And, if I tried it, who knows what would happen? Perhaps tumble forward and end up careening down head first not able to grab hold of anything – impossible to slow my descent. And perhaps even gouging my ski tips or ski edges into the snow crust, wrenching my ankles, maybe my knees?

Perhaps I can side-slip . . . line up my skis parallel to each other, but then I'd be trying savagely to force my uphill ski edge into the mountain. Isn't that what I've been told *not* to do?

Or, could I traverse back and forth? But that would take forever. Each trip would yield me a descent of only a couple of feet.

If I opt to fall, just pull right out of my ski bindings so I'd be free of my slippery ski runners beneath me and try to literally walk down the mountain, who's to say I wouldn't instead end up in a spread-eagle sprawl, rolling and tumbling, unable to control my descent?

I look out at the fall line and the steepness of the descent grips me all over again. Things don't look good. Not good at all.

I lean forward, my poles rammed into the snow on either side of me, my uphill ski edge biting into the up-mountain snow. I strain to see through the gathering darkness, to assess the configuration of the drops and rises ahead of me, and I become starkly aware that my goggles are steamed. I'm looking through mist. Everything's turned to white fog.

I'm crying like a baby, that's why.

I pull down on my ski goggles and twist them around to the back of my head . . . "gotta get rid of 'em. They're no help in this light."

I try to wipe my eyes clear but my ski gloves are caked with snow. 'What's left to do if I can't see? Just *feel* my way down this mountain?' Suddenly my anxiety has morphed into terror.

Tentatively, I flex myself on my skis – only slightly. What I want to know is if my knees and ankles feel strong enough to be bent and agile long enough to hold my skis, aligned, straight ahead of me. They've got to be if I'm to take what is fast becoming a really frightening unknown. But I know I can't stop now.

I can't tell if I'm muttering out loud, but it's for sure the voices in my head are shouting at fever pitch.

'Yeh, yeh,' I'm trying to yell back at them . . . 'I know. I know there's got to be a way.' But those voices keep up their jeering. "The others made it down, how about you?"

I wanna yell back, "I oughta be able to do the same; I could in the past," only to have still another voice overlay my weak attempts to bolster my courage, 'Yeh, but they know how. . . they have the strength and agility, but look at you.'

Cautiously, I straighten up. I inhale the cold mountain air. For a moment it's soothing to me, but then I realize I'm sweating. I'm drenched.

Still, I force myself to flex my knees and to bend down, and I'm gripping my ski poles for dear life, exactly as I have – ever since my youth on these slopes —been told *not* to do. But to *not* cling and to *not* grasp at anything that might offer security calls for an awful lot more courage than I have at this moment. With all the will I can muster, I try to force the fear out of me and drive it away. Force it out of me like willing a thunderous avalanche to stop mid-air and settle into silence . . . to make my raging fear somehow small and nonthreatening. . . a task – I know – to be far easier to think than to do. And in the face of this, my body mocks me. Every muscle, regardless of how I will them otherwise, feels like they're ratcheting tighter and tighter.

I take in a breath. . . I lean forward . . .

'That's right. That's the way. Now go limber.'

'Is that still one more voice, as if there aren't enough already? But this one's somehow different. This one has a steady quality to it. More authoritative. More in command.'

Then from someplace long ago, I sense I know this voice. From when I was a little kid. 'Use the knees like springs.' The voice is calm. 'Let them absorb the shocks.' The hysterical clamor that nearly unhinged me earlier gives way, and in this silent space, I hear: 'Are you listening to me?' If you are, then lean out – you hear – lean out!'

I'm thinking to myself that I'm not brave enough or crazy enough to carry this out. Like being asked to become insane in order to become sane, to deliberately and with intention contradict my intuition. I cower as I look out over that awesome snow-packed expanse below me.

Feeling my way along, there's a sudden shift. My skis go into a steep drop. In no time, I'm swooping precipitously downward, only to be met with another rise. Then more.

'Not a mogul field,' I gasp. 'How can I make out the contours of moguls in all this white on white on white?'

'Go for the rhythm."

'There it is again. That calm, Masterful voice. 'Go for the rhythm, Child.'

I try to crouch low, straining to see where one hillock stops and another starts, trying to absorb the change in the terrain, then suddenly I soar to the top of another mogul, then down, around and up again, and over . . .

'Maintain speed. Keep control,' I'm saying to myself – now like two voices blending into one. 'I've taken moguls before, so I can take them again,' I think through clenched teeth.

And sure enough, it comes back to me. . . the slower I go, the less my control. The more my momentum, the easier it is to pick up on the rhythm. And there it is: down, around and up and over. Down, around, up and over. Right then, clearly, in that moment, I realize I'm not favoring my uphill ski.

'Hey, I'm not hugging the up-mountain!' I wanna shout out. 'Not dragging at the snow with my poles either.' Down, around, up and over. 'Look at this. I'm not cutting into the snow with my ski edges. I've got control.' Down, around, up and over. 'And, I'm leaning out! I'm really leaning out over the mountain!'

I begin to play with the sensation . . . not enough to let myself become reckless and spin out . . . just enough to begin to grasp the dance of it.

Cautiously, I try to keep my weight over the down-hill ski. Timidly, I keep leaning out. I catch a glimpse of the frozen solitude stretching beneath me.

Suddenly I feel tired all over again. Really tired. "Is it my age? But I'm not going to give in to it," I set my jaw, and somehow my resolve energizes me.

For that one instant I'm pumped just enough that for a split second I let myself look up. That barest glimpse tells me I'm seeing high into the darkening, domed sky. I see right through it and beyond. I see it's a heavenly place – diamonded with early evening stars – clear and cloudless. Without effort, I take in a huge gulp . . . of pure serenity.

Then I let out a howl, and with it flies my tension.

'Push ahead!' I hear it again. And, I resume the rhythm: Down, around, up, and over. Again and again. Carefully, methodically, keeping up my momentum, I am giving myself to the mountain . . . giving myself up to the unknown . . .

Freelance writer and adventurer extraordinaire.

PINK SLIP

Rosie Loew

I was fired. And, I'm only 61. Maybe it shouldn't have been such a shock with the economy in the state it's in now. This is a whole new experience for me. I've never even been unemployed, except when I personally chose to be. Since graduating from high school, and with my friends from college, we'd all easily found jobs and fascinating ones at that. There was no problem supporting myself and taking courses, racking up licenses and certificates. I was so credentialed I could hold down more than one substantial job at a time. I seriously felt I had it made.

But that was then. This is now.

At the time I got my pink slip, I was sharing the house I'd purchased a half a dozen years ago. House mate, Carolyn, came to rent from me soon after I'd bought it. We enjoyed each other. Had interests in common. Shared expenses. Made life work – gloriously, I thought.

Then, could you ever have guessed it, Carolyn McCormack, the consummate professional and my friend of nearly five years, just two days after me, was also fired from her high level position. She'd enjoyed a solid place in what had been a flourishing, highly productive start-up firm. The CFO to be exact.

I was admittedly in shock – first for my own plight, and then for Carolyn's as well. When she came into the house that afternoon, her file boxes in tow, she and I found ourselves in the living room staring at each other, mute. The shock was so great we felt every emotion you could imagine, and on top of this, it's coming close to the end of the month with the usual bills to pay and neither of us now has an income.

"I don't know what we're facing here in terms of our options," I said. But I was met with no clear-eyed response. It was as if I was talking through Carolyn. It felt like all I had thought Carolyn to be had somehow dissolved – misted away. There seemed nothing I could hook into.

"Look," I said finally, we have next week until the first of the month. We can each pull together a plan, but right now, I'm feeling an awful fatigue. Maybe a little rest, then to the planning . . ."

But before I could finish my sentence, Carolyn erupts, "How could they do this to me?" She's literally wailing. "You just don't do this to a MacCormack," and she appears to slip sideways into hysteria, then wavers and slides the other way into anger. Then she throws one of her file boxes across the living room floor, and she flings herself full-body onto the couch. Pummeling the couch pillows, scratching her long, manicured finger nails down the couch back, pulling off her shoes and throwing them all the way across the room slamming them against the front door.

"Carolyn," I managed to shout. "This doesn't get you anyplace. Sit down. Quiet yourself. I'll get you a cup of tea, then, we'll discuss the situation."

"There's nothing to discuss." Carolyn was relentless. "I spent a chunk of my savings on my new BMW. I've got insurance premiums I won't be able to meet. I'm staring at a massive dental bill and my company insurance plan is kaput. Just like that. All my benefits are cut off. I got no buyout package because the company has gone under. Two years to go 'til Social Security. No retirement. The company buy-in program is dead in the water and we're told there will likely be no recouping our investment . . . and just last month I cleared out my reserves, cashed in my stocks and put it all in this frigging company, and now I have nothing to show for it. Nothing.

"Not so fast, Carolyn. I'm in a far worse situation than you," and I'm thinking to myself how to calm this adolescent temper tantrum I'm forced into with this suddenly petulant, one-time high powered CFO. "Look, my greatest asset is my house, this house right here . . . sunk everything into this place and the way I'm figuring it I can probably hang on, with a roof over my head, for about three months, maybe four – max. During these few days I've been out of work, I've begun looking into my options. What I'm learning is that I stand to lose not only my house but everything I'm making payments on. I stand to see my credit rating plummet. Then talk about a slippery slope. Who knows where this will stop. But first, if you don't want some tea, and you don't want to discuss our situations calmly, then as for me, what I'm going to do right now is go to my room, close the blinds, and I'm going to sleep on this. Then next, I'm going to take my yellow pad and begin a list of how I can dig myself out of this pit. If you want to, I invite you to participate."

Sleep? Are you out of your mind? To-do lists? Ah come on. I wanna sue those bastards, take them to the cleaners . . ." and the tirade went on while I climbed the stairs, went to my room, closed the door and turned inward.

Amazing, I thought, how this A-1 competent gal when everything is going her way, does just fine. But suddenly when the tough times come, I watch while she morphs into a mass of seething emotions. And, quite frankly, I wonder about all this. How could she have made it through an upscale upbringing, attended the best schools, and when an obstacle is tossed in her way she has so little to meet it with.

༄

"You're going to do what?" Carolyn fairly screeches at me.

"Yes, that's right. I am, and you can bring home some money too if you want to come along."

"There's no way you'll find me doing that or anything like it."

"That's your choice, I respond in an even tone of voice.

"Well, it certainly is," she hisses back and I leave Carolyn sitting on the couch polishing her nails while I meet up with the rest of the team. We set off to clean offices during evening hours at minimum wage plus one dollar, but hey, look at it this way, when I return I will have close to a hundred dollars in my pocket . . . doesn't take a lot of thinking to make that work for me if I keep my snob-level in check."

༄

In time, just as I feared and expected, my major asset fell into foreclosure. I have no parents to help me out, no resources to fall back on, even though I've tried to be careful not to live beyond my means. My problem is that I have not set aside anything for emergency needs. I, along with so many like me, lived my income to the fullest. After all, we are of the Boomer generation. We're the enviable product of parents who wanted us to 'have it all.' We've been through the self-esteem movement, and we're technical wizards. If something touches our fancy, what is there to keep us from acquiring it and taking it in hand *now*? Delayed gratification isn't even a part of our vocabulary, in fact it's gobble-de-gook and has no place in our world.

⸻

Carolyn finally set about to pack her bags and I figure she'll be moving out – especially when I see her tossing her four-inch stilettos into her Magellan top-of-the-line luggage. Who am I to stop her from heaving them at her Uncle Joe's door, particularly if he dares ask her to babysit for his kids. She'd gone through her parents' generosity but they were then nearing elder-home age. She'd worn out her friends and ex-colleagues. As for both of us, with the loss of our jobs, we lost our medical benefits. While Carolyn flew from one rage to another, I turned silent, only to come up diagnosed with a painful case of Shingles, "Stress related," the doctor said. Well, duh…!

Carolyn moved out and I didn't hear from her. In the meantime, I managed to put together what earnings I could to get COBRA coverage, a policy set up by unemployment insurance and available for a three year period.

The final allotted time for unemployment came and went both slowly and quickly. For all my attempts to find work, I was not successful. I was interviewed many times. Every time I was told I was qualified but was never offered a job. It was especially difficult for me when I noticed the interviewers were half my age.

I had no more savings; my credit card was maxed out. Then one day, quite by coincidence, from a conversation with a casual friend, I learned about the Easter Seal program, a New York City Title V program established as a Federal Law by Lyndon Johnson back in 1967. It's federally funded by the US Department of Labor and is an employment and jobs training program for those over fifty-five. I jumped at this.

Today, I can say I'm deeply thankful I happened upon this program. I've learned up-to-date computer skills, and made use of the job placement opportunities. I now earn enough to pay rent, food, credit card debt and cover transportation. Then I put away as much as I can of what's left over. Of course, it's not much. But when it comes to my budget, I take it seriously.

"Pardon me, but is that you, Carolyn?"

The lady I address looks up at me, now far wearier than I'd ever seen her. "Yea, it's me," she says, "and what high-handed stuff do you have to talk to me about today? I guess you can gather from what you're seeing here no one will honor my credentials. They see how qualified I am, then look away."

It doesn't need to be like this, Carolyn . . ."

"You mean you can direct me to some toilets that need cleaning; well, that's not for me. Even if it would be better than the way I'm living now."

"But it is. Let me help you."

"Ya know, friend, when I'm respected for who I am and what I've already accomplished, that's when I'll give them a chance with me. They can start me at the level where I left off. And, nothing less."

Saddened, I say good-bye, worried about Carolyn's health living in shelters at night and walking the streets during the day. I grieve and feel deeply concerned about her – and so many now in her situation.

As for myself, what I can say for sure is that besides the fortunate opportunity to have found this particular Title V program, I have to add that I am also fortunate to have faith to fall back on.

Back some years, I began to take my spiritual life seriously. When I had money, I used it to make trips to study with Tibetan monks. I learned Vipassana meditation, the technique that is said to have liberated the Buddha. Through all of these trials I've recently experienced, what has kept me calm, what has kept my mind orderly and my thinking focused is the result of my spiritual practice. For example, what could be better than adopting the very practical point of view – yet apparently esoteric to some folks – that whether I sleep on straw, or on velvet, I view this as *change*, not poverty, nor wealth, just change. Because, bottom line, it just doesn't matter.

I'm sorry I can't talk with Carolyn about these things, but perhaps there will be a time.

What I've learned from all this is the re-affirmation that discipline with flexibility together with a willing heart has a way of carrying me a mighty long way.

Rosie Loew lives in New York City where she has spent many years working in the real estate business. Her life's focus has been spirituality. She has had one other story published entitled *Near and Dear* in *Transformation of the Heart*.

"Twenty years from now you will be more disappointed by the things you didn't do than by the ones you did do. So throw off the bowlines. Sail away from the safe harbor."

Mark Twain

THE LAST SAIL

Janet Hines

It would be only the two of us today, Doug and I, sailing a boat once filled with the laughter of our girls and the voices of our friends. Of course, we wouldn't speak of those times, acutely aware of our current, uncertain relationship, nor would we talk of the future. We would sail in silence, joined by familiar tasks, yet each of us very much alone and now in our senior years. Sailing had been an important activity in our lives for how long now? Fourteen, fifteen years or so, but never really a part of me, never the passion I hoped for, never the answer I expected it to be. I knew my sailing days were about to end, and in some ways I would miss them, but not enough to seek out another boat or someone else with whom to sail it.

There wasn't much breeze that morning. Palm trees at the marina entrance barely stirred, their fronds limp in the warm, humid air. A lone mynah bird, scratching in the dry grass under the trees, paused to lift his head and screech in warning as I walked along the sandy path. I smiled at him as I shifted the canvas bag on my shoulder and continued slowly toward the marina office, admiring from a distance the red hibiscus hedge against the weathered walls of the building.

Leaving the path to walk down the wooden dock to the boat, I was in no hurry, wanting to hold on to the sights and sounds of a place I usually didn't take the time to see. I recognized the familiar feelings of unease I had for so long associated with sailing. There had been too many close calls, too many tense days sailing under small craft warnings, too many things to go wrong.

Owning a sailboat was Doug's dream, not mine, and while I enjoyed it some of the time, more often I didn't. I'd learned early in our marriage that Doug loved the water and especially sailing. Born in Tahiti, he'd learned to swim at an early age, swam for his high school team, then for Princeton, and was as comfortable in the water as I was on land. Our friends, Sam and Jan Palmer, had a lovely wooden-hulled sailboat and early in our marriage, we'd meet them in Balboa and spend Saturday afternoons sailing around the bay. Later, after we'd lived in Hawaii for several years, it came as no surprise when Doug suggested he would like a sailboat of his own.

Doug had finished hosing off the boat by the time I reached it. The hatch was open and the cooler with our lunch and drinks was obviously aboard and stowed in the cabin. The mainsail cover was off and the bag holding the jib lay on the forward deck. I had let Doug off at the marina gate, parked the van, and deliberately prolonged my solitary walk to the slip, knowing he'd have the boat ready to take out when I got there. We knew our jobs well by this time, and mine was to assist the captain. Doug was the captain, he laid down the rules. He steered the course. There was no mutiny, and no hidden agenda on this ship. What went on at home was another matter.

I stood on the dock and looked at the boat. The white hull glistened in the sunlight, a wide band of blue circling its sides like a ribbon. Teak trim softened the hard surfaces of fiberglass and stainless steel and the tall aluminum mast towered over the deck and cockpit. Thick nylon lines ran up the length of the mast, their fittings beating a faint tattoo against the metal as the boat rocked gently with the motion of the tide. There was a wide, flat deck forward, a generous cockpit and a nicely fitted cabin below. Officially the boat was known as a Columbia 26, but to us it was called by its name, Kalipe, painted in bold black letters on the stern.

This wasn't our first boat, nor was it our second. It was the third in a series of Kalipes. When Doug initially broached the subject of buying a sailboat, it was understood that the boat would be modest, not too large and something he could sail alone without a crew. The girls were young then, about four, five and seven, and we both knew my opportunities for sailing would be limited. Doug spent time searching for just the right boat, and, after several months of following ads and visiting boat yards, found exactly what he wanted, a twelve-foot, fiberglass boat with a varnished spruce mast. We were eager to launch it and try it out, but first it needed a name. We agonized over that name and I don't remember who came up with the final choice, but we'd decided that it should be Hawaiian or at least sound Hawaiian and it should mean something to us. We also wanted the name to be one word and not obvious. We chose the name Kalipe and were amused when asked the English translation for this unfamiliar Hawaiian word. "Guess," we'd say, but no one figured it out. KA- LI- PE, Katy, Lisa and Peggy, our three daughters.

I climbed aboard, stowed my bag in the cabin and busied myself with lines and seat cushions while Doug attached the outboard motor to the stern. We wouldn't raise the sails until well beyond the narrow channel and hidden treachery of the island's coral reef. We cast off, and with the motor on low throttle, slowly made our way out of the marina and into the channel, increasing speed as we left land behind. Doug stood at the tiller, guiding the boat as I sat at my usual post on the deck, leaning against the mast. The wind picked up, and I felt it on my face and in my hair. I could smell the island scent of flowers, salt and ocean, a fragrance laden with memories – in later years, to be an unbidden reminder of a bittersweet past. I watched as the water changed from light to dark green, green blue and then the pure blue of lapis, my color, the color of the stone in jewelry Doug had given me, the color of my eyes he once said. As we approached the channel opening, I heard the thundering crash of waves breaking across the reef. The surf rose in great, curling walls of water, crests boiling with white foam, tossing rainbow-hued mist high in the air. I stood, transfixed by the energy of the tidal pull, absorbed by its power, not heeding my usual caution as I swayed from side to side with the motion of the boat. The unhappiness that had been surrounding me for the past few months was forgotten; I felt only the wind, the sun and the sea.

Doug sometimes sailed the first Kalipe alone, launching from the boat ramp at Hawaii Kai, sailing toward Niu until he could see our house perched high above the valley floor. Usually, though, we packed up mats and towels, a picnic lunch, sand toys, boat gear and the girls, and drove, with Kalipe on her trailer behind the car, to Kailua beach on the windward side of the island. The beach was wide with white, fine sand, warm water and gentle, lapping waves – a perfect beach for the girls and a perfect place to launch a small boat. I was content to watch as Kalipe skimmed the water with her captain at the helm or more often with one small crewmember at his side. "Me next, my turn," one of the girls would call out, dropping her shovel and running to the water's edge as Doug maneuvered the boat to shore. I didn't often have a turn unless the five of us got into the boat together, a logistical puzzle of tangled arms and legs, but I didn't mind. I understood the importance of Doug's connection to boats and water and knew that sailing somehow eased the inner struggle I sensed beneath his calm exterior.

I turn as Doug cuts off the motor, the sudden silence a relief. I remove the bungees from the mainsail while he stores the engine under a cockpit seat. We move efficiently as we exchange places, he at the mast and I at the tiller, avoiding contact or meeting one another's eyes. I look up as he begins to raise the voluminous sail, shielding my eyes from the glare on its bright surface. Doug had changed to a red and white pareao, its long wrapped skirt lifting and flapping in the wind. Both his chest and feet are bare. He balances expertly on the deck as he pulls steadily on the line, watching the sail slowly advance to the top of the mast, his profile is clearly outlined against the sky. The shape of his head, the strength in his shoulders and arms, the grace in his movements proclaim his Polynesian heritage, informing those who knew what to look for, that this is an island boy. "The Tahitian prince," I thought, acknowledging his ancestors, who in their great canoes were the first to sail into Hawaiian waters and set their feet on Hawaiian soil. Though neither born nor raised in Hawaii, he belongs in these islands, while I, who secretly long for cool, dry air and the oak shaded hills of California, never will.

I begin to pull up the slack on the line and wind it around the winch as Doug takes the tiller, the sail luffing and the boom swinging wildly from side to side until we turn to catch the wind. With a burst of energy the sail fills and the boat, like a horse out of the gate, speeds forward. Gusts of wind from the valleys of the Koolau range push against the sail and the boat heels sharply, its starboard rail only inches above the water. Swells slap against the hull as the bow rises and falls with the rhythm of the open ocean, and I close my mind to everything but the moment and the giddy exhilaration of the ride.

When the first Kalipe was deemed too small to continue service as the family's main source of recreation, she was sold. I detected a resigned sadness in Doug as he put the boat up for sale, but we didn't discuss his feelings, just as we never touched on anything more than the day-to-day routine of keeping family life going. Calendars, chores and responsibilities were attended to faithfully, but matters of the heart and soul began to be carefully avoided until finally they withered and were buried in places where they couldn't easily be found. Not long after the first little boat was sold, we found another in a boatyard out in the industrial area toward Pearl Harbor. The new boat was 18 feet long, had the requisite small cabin, an adequate cockpit, and a retractable centerboard instead of a keel. It was green, as I recall, but I can't remember much more than that. This second boat was called Kalipe too, just like the first, and we stored it in a makeshift slip in Kaneohe Bay.

I enjoy bay sailing with its calm winds and interesting things to look at on shore, but in time there came a sameness to our sailing days and the girls began to find excuses not to go. None of us really cared about that boat and in time we knew its days were numbered. Eventually, with no regrets, it was sold. Then the hunt began for the serious boat, the one to accommodate all of us with comfort, sail out into the ocean, maybe to an outer island, the one to fulfill dreams and bind us together. Were we asking too much of that boat, deceiving ourselves that it, along with a new job and a bigger house, would fix a broken family?

Doug points the boat toward Diamond Head, the views of the coastline glorious in the late morning light. The tall, green Koolaus stand as sentinels beyond the beaches and neighborhoods of Honolulu, their sides carved into deep seams and valleys by rain-laden streams. Glittering sparks of sunlight dance from glass paned windows on shore and the great banyans, monkeypods, kukuis, and clusters of palms mask the concrete and asphalt of Honolulu's relentless progress. As we approach Waikiki, the rainbow sided Hilton dwarfed its neighbors on a beach once dominated by the Royal Hawaiian, Halekulani and Moana, *grand dames* now barely visible among high-rise newcomers. Long, slow rollers sweep toward the beach and I can see tiny figures dotting the golden stretch of sand along the water's edge. I sit at the bow of the boat, dangling my feet as I rest against the railing, absorbed in my thoughts. I think about Doug and the remains of our marriage. It is only a matter of time, I admit to myself. Why am I hanging on? This second try at a marriage, long over, had worked for a while. To be fair, Doug has tried to put it right. He has been dutiful in his attentions to the girls and me, but, though physically living in our house, his mind and heart are elsewhere. I don't have to be told he is seeing Susan again. I know, and with the knowledge comes relief. The hurt is not less, but the ability to let go, I know will help to begin the healing, enabling me to find a life of my own.

I never saw the third and final Kalipe again. It was listed on Doug's side of the ledger when we politely sat down with lawyers to divide the spoils of our twenty-year marriage. I got the furniture and he got the boat, an appropriate division I thought at the time. I later learned that not long after Doug's marriage to Susan, Kalipe was sold and exchanged for a horse. (Susan decided she didn't care for sailing, but she'd always dreamed of owning a horse.) We all have dreams and when we love someone very much, we often sacrifice our own to make the other's come true.

I hadn't given much thought to my own dreams during the years of husband and children. My job was to see to theirs. I didn't know my life had been on hold then, willing to be an observer, waiting for something to change. After the divorce, my *re-entry* into a new life didn't happen right away, but once it began I was suddenly alive, recapturing all of the feelings I'd so carefully hidden throughout the years. The protective layers concealing my emotions peeled away, revealing the sense of self I thought I'd lost.

I look back and find that memories of my sailing days are fond ones, and to my surprise, so are those of my marriage to Doug. Blame and regrets have faded, and if I allow it, only the best times remain. Just as I traded a boat for a houseful of furniture, I traded a marriage for a piece of paper and a future full with dreams.

Los Angeles, San Francisco and Honolulu are the settings for Jan Hines' collection of personal essays and short stories. Her interest in events that shape and change lives is reflected in her memoir, *The Glass Half Full.* Ms. Hines currently lives in Solvang, CA.

JUST FOLLOWING ORDERS

Barbara Lydecker Crane

The doc advises, *Slow down*.
Miranda, ninety, drags her heels;
she maintains full-speed-ahead.

The doc insists, *Don't drive in town*.
Miranda smiles, spins her wheels
at midnight on the beach, instead.

The doc decrees, with bark and frown,
Put your feet up after meals.
She does, by standing on her head.

I've published two chapbooks, *Zero Granitas*, White Violet Press, 2012 and ALPHABETRICS (for children), Daffydowndilly Press, 2013. In the US, my poems have appeared in *Atlantic Review, Comstock Review, Light Quarterly* and *Measure* among others; in the UK, in *Angle, The Flea* and 14 by 14, and in eight anthologies.

A DIFFERENT FAREWELL

Doris Thome

A fall to the floor of their retirement home apartment starts an eight day journey for my ninety-two-year old father, my eighty-five year old mother and our family. Dad has suffered a major stroke. Assisted by staff, as well as myself, his daughter and long-time Hospice nurse, Dad is transferred to the nursing unit.

My parents have been specific in their wishes to avoid heroic measures. Legal papers to this effect have been signed and their doctor knows and agrees with their wishes. Many think having a medical directive is all that is needed. Not so. The patient's physician must agree to honor the patient's wishes. Is their designated physician available at the time? On vacation? Is some other physician on-call? Until there is a current doctor's order, medical facilities follow their protocol of implementing lifesaving methods. Your busy doctor can't be expected to remember; it's up to each of us or the designated person to hunt down the physician and have the nurse take the order.

Following his stroke Dad is unable to move, talk, or swallow. I remind Mom of their medical directives. "Mom, you and Dad gave me power of attorney, but we've come to that cross in the road. You've told me many times that you do not want your lives extended: no suctioning, no feeding tubes, or machines. The only chance to keep Dad alive is to feed him by inserting a tube into his stomach. His stroke is severe. Do you want to stick to the plan or try to keep him alive?"

I know what Mom's answer will be but I want to give her a chance to rethink their decision. "I can't do that to him." Mom says. "I wouldn't want that done to me. No, I don't think we should change a thing."

I move to the side of the hospital bed and communicate with Dad as best I can. His lopsided smile is a painful reminder of what fate has dealt him, but it lets me know that he recognizes me. His left hand is strong and he clutches my hand so tightly that I realize he's frightened.

"Dad, it's Jessie; you've had a stroke. Not being able to move or talk must be terribly frustrating. I know you're uncomfortable. I'm going to call Dr. Netzer to get something for pain. But first, I need to ask you a question. I want you to answer by squeezing my hand, one squeeze for yes, two squeezes for no. Do you understand?"

His stare is penetrating. His full concentration is on my face as he squeezes my hand once. I smile at him. He is lucid. His thinking, again clear.

"Dad, I want to make sure we do what you want. Do you want to be kept alive on a feeding tube?" The double squeeze comes practically before I finish.

I kiss him on his cheek, proud of my parents for their strong stance and for not buckling at this time of crisis. A tear drops on his shoulder; I didn't realize I was crying.

"Mom will stay with you. I'll call the Doctor and be right back."

Dr Netzer gives the order for comfort measures only, medicate for pain, no tubes, NPO (nothing per oral) and reposition Q2 (every two hours).

Mom and I both stay at the bedside. We take turns. Mom is at a loss to make herself understood and this makes Daddy upset. With me, our exchanges consist of an easy rapport. As an RN, I try to demonstrate, hoping Mom will pick up what works and why. I always tell my father who I am and remind him of our one-handed link. Periodically, I moisten his mouth, wash his face and hands, rub his back or change his position, always asking his permission. I never touch my father without his knowing I am there and visualizing his recognition of me. Many staff members forget to do this and if I am around I ask to help, again demonstrating something they probably know, but perhaps don't bother doing because it takes time.

On the fourth day, Daddy slips into a coma. We wait. Since hearing is believed to be the last sense to go, I don't change my routine. I let him know I am with him. I bathe his body, change his diaper, and reposition him. I talk about our lives, what he means to me, and how much I will miss him. I remind him of some of my childhood memories, hoping that he hears them especially as I laugh, and this time I let my tears fall where they may.

The sixth morning, Dad wakes. His eyes travel the perimeter of the room in which he is being cared for. Disbelief shows in his expression. Dad shuts his eyes and tears slide down his cheeks.

I lift his left hand in mine, "Yes, you're still here," I tell him "It's not easy to let go, is it?"

Two squeezes. He rolls his eyes and sighs deeply.

"Dad, do you sometimes see your Mama and your Papa?"

Quickly I receive a single squeeze accompanied by a puzzled expression.

"Are you unsure of where to go?"

One squeeze. Yes.

"Did something confuse you?"

One squeeze.

"Was it a bright light?"

Daddy's eyes dart side to side and his brow furrows. I see fear and doubt in his eyes, but then he gives me one long and very hard, single squeeze.

"It's not clear?"

A quick squeeze.

"Kind of confusing?"

Another squeeze.

"Don't be afraid, Daddy. It will clear. Keep going. Everyone will be there to meet you, your mama and your papa. Your old friend, Heinz, will be waiting for you, your brothers and sisters, all your family and friends are expecting you. You know the best part?"

Dad's eyes open wide with curiosity.

"When you get there, you won't be ninety-two. You won't have had a stroke. You will walk tall, be strong and look just the way each person remembers you and they will look the way you remember them."

Dad calms. It feels so wonderful to again be able to connect with my father. Hours later he slips into another coma. We spend the day waiting. I continue to reposition him, noting the cooling of his body, seeing signs that my father's life is diminishing. I speak in hushed tones as I stroke and comfort him or perhaps these gestures are for me. Not that he can feel, but I continue. I even massage his scalp.

Mom sits in the corner and watches. I know I should turn my attention to Mother. Is she grieving at a loss, or perhaps angry because it's so easy for me? It's not, but she has mentioned this to me before when Daddy's intermittent dementia irritated her or when his responses toward me were lucid and our exchanges fun.

The darkening sky and the clock lets me know it is seven p.m. "Mom, I need to shower, change my clothes and eat something homemade. Eating here or eating out day after day doesn't agree with my stomach. Too much salt or additives, whatever— I need fresh vegetables, lots of water, something simple. I'm heading home now."

"Are you coming back tonight, or in the morning?"

"I'll return later tonight," I assure her.

I make the long descent down the mountains, fly past the tunnel and rest stop, make the curve to drive down highway 101, mountains to my left and ocean to my right. Halfway home I become distracted. Whether vision or sound is first, I cannot tell.

Suddenly, a whoosh of wind like energy as loud as a locomotive catching up to me. I am in the fast lane traveling at a speed of 72 mph and next to me just off the road parallel with my driver's window, a four-foot ball of glowing light slows to keep abreast. I feel a lightness. Euphoria fills me.

"Dad, you made it," I say aloud. "Good for you!"

The radiating ball and its tendrils of displaced wind, veer further off the road, then speed up over an open field and swoosh up the verdant hillside. Then, gone. My clock reads 7:24.

I slow and continue my drive home. More relaxed now, grateful my father is no longer afraid or suffering, I'm joyous he let me know.

As I enter my Santa Barbara home, the phone is ringing. I'm sure it is Mom. Her first words: "Dad died."

"I know. At 7:24."

"How did you know the time?"

I know my mother doesn't comprehend, and I can't make her understand. All I can say is: It happens this way sometimes. I've seen this over and over again with my hospice patients.

"He said goodbye, Mom; I felt him leave."

Doris Thome: See Bio following *Final Adventure*.

WHAT A SHAME, SHE HAS SUCH A PRETTY FACE

Kathy Marden

A sad little girl still resides within me, but we have become friends and we remind ourselves that we are fine and good and strong no matter what we weigh.

You see, the one thing my actress mother feared, the one thing that was unacceptable was to be fat, and suddenly, inexplicably it was happening to me. I couldn't stop it. I kept growing – the wrong way. I was going through puberty, gaining inches and pounds instead of taking them off. I tried to deny it, but then I would catch a glimpse of myself in a store window and hardly recognize my politely described "chubby body".

Shopping trips became torturous. Lane Bryant loomed. They had clothes for the young lady who was "chubby." How I hated that place, but it was my only choice after spending a mortifying afternoon in the regular department of the regular store, tears rolling down my face and pretty dresses bunched up in a mess on the floor, none of them to be mine.

Incidents of humiliation and pain began to come more and more frequently. Going to dancing school where the boys and girls lined up to face each other was worse than going to my dentist who didn't believe in Novocain. I remember one day in class I wore a beautiful white net dress covered in tiny blue flowers. The teacher called me over to help demonstrate a step. When she turned to the whole class and said, "Isn't she a lovely dancer? Too bad she's not a little lighter." I wanted to die right there.

You have to understand, my mother and father were actors. I didn't know that was a strange thing to be. I didn't know there were gossip columns and movie magazines that talked about how often actors got divorced. I didn't know what divorce meant until my dad left, and my mother became a single mother. There were no support groups then or accolades for her survival spirit, just fear, loneliness, bills to be paid and two little girls.

So I stopped being a little girl and became her friend, her helper and, at times, he mother. She would look at me with her big, beautiful movie star eyes and remind me, "You're the oldest. I need your help."

"Take the phone messages; never wake me from a nap."

"Do you like this dress I am wearing?"

"Do I look pretty?"

"Am I too fat?"

What an oddity the three of us were. How different I felt. My mother was not only divorced, she was a Democrat, a Unitarian, she smoked Lucky Strike cigarettes, and she said "Dammit" when she was mad. I was so embarrassed.

My friends had Ozzie and Harriett moms. Mine was asleep when I left for school and took a nap when I came home. It was lonely and scary to come home to the house with a sleeping woman. I prayed the phone wouldn't ring. Those decisions were excruciating. If I made the wrong one and woke her, I faced a wild eyed screaming banshee. If I didn't wake her, I faced an angry tirade. Her agent was the most important call. I knew that. But sometimes she was mad at him for not getting her enough work, so then I shouldn't wake her. How to know? How to judge? I hated to hear the phone ring.

There were no milk and cookies waiting for me when I got home. There were no cookies anyway. She was always dieting, her little calorie book and white pad next to her plate. But I found other ways to fill up. I could binge on sliced oranges and lots and lots of cinnamon sugar on buttered toast. Or peanut butter cracker towers, built with the care of the finest bricklayer.

Pretty soon people began to notice. I would hear them talking.

"Wait until she goes through puberty, it'll come off."

"What a shame, she has such a pretty face."

I had become a "problem." My weight had become an "issue." Something had to be done. My mother had a special doctor for every part of her body. She was a great believer in the "Specialist." So, she found a doctor who specialized in adolescent weight problems.

He said, "You probably won't lose the weight but here's a diet. Come back in a week."

It took me all summer to lose thirty pounds, but I did it. I stood on the corner the first day of school with a new haircut and my first-ever straight skirt in bright, bold red. I was waiting for my life to begin. I knew that it had to be different, that I would be popular, and boys would like me.

I had no idea as I stood there expectantly in the early morning air that the fat little girl inside me would not just disappear with the pounds, or a new haircut, or new clothes. I had no idea how powerful the memory of my former fat self was. I had no idea that the fear of being that way again would drive me to obsessive lengths in my attempt to control the demon hunger within.

I had no idea how separate I would feel from other women, women I perceived had never felt so ashamed and humiliated.

I had no idea that the scar tissue would be so thick and would take so many years to soften and fall off.

But there has certainly been a softening of that scar tissue, although, in truth, it never really goes away altogether. I have spent too many years, too many hours agonizing about one pound, a slave to the scale. If my weight was down, it was a good day, and otherwise I was a failure.

This is what I have realized: it doesn't matter how much I weigh, what size pants I wear or how many hours I've exercised. What I have learned that matters most is how I love and how I care about those I love. What matters is laughing, living life to the fullest and enjoying each day. I've learned I can quiet the inner voice the way I calm my grandchildren. And the greatest irony of all is that they don't even care how fat, thin, tall, short, flabby or fit I am. They love me unconditionally, as I am finally learning to love myself.

Kathy Marden is a practicing psychotherapist and a sometime community actress. She started writing a few years ago having landed in a memoir writing class through the local adult education program. She has found writing to be therapeutic, exhilarating, frustrating and powerful. She has had one other story published in *Panik: Candid Stories of Life Altering Experiences Surrounding Pregnancy*.

THE YELLOW BATHTUB

J. C. Reinhart

"Ah, the perfect luxury of it," she sighed, obviously delighted. "Just think, a Saturday night in nothing but comfort. No demands. No interruptions."

I was comfortable being at home alone with Mom. "Go. Shoo now," I encouraged my brother and his family. "I came to help you in just this way. You go on. Have a good evening. Don't give a thought to us. Don't even bother to call in. I'll do just fine."

I was glad to be able to help out. My brother was the primary Care Giver for our mother, now in her 90s. He needed a break and so this, as one of my several trips a year from my home in California back to the place I grew up I in Ohio, offered him just that.

I watched his car lights as he backed out of the driveway, not knowing I was about to experience one of the most curious, arduous, yet strangely exhilarating events of my adult life.

"Come along, Dear," Mother called to me from the bathroom. She had gestured for me to gather her towels and personal paraphernalia for her very personal spa evening . . . "Alone," she emphasized.

I respect what she says, but what about my own presence? I'm wondering. But Mother gives no signals that I'd be an interference, not now with fragrant bath salts filling her senses while the hot water fills her happy, yellow ceramic bath tub.

Yellow is a favorite color of Mom's. There is the yellow bath tub, the yellow sink, and yellow toilet - like spring daffodils against the green tiled walls she had installed in the bathroom. The house even boasts yellow cabinets in the kitchen, and even a happy, yellow kitchen tile floor.

I would wonder now and then . . . Maybe all this yellowness has had something to do with the bouts of depression she suffered, depression mingled with migraines that could send her to bed for several days at a time.

But the whys and the wherefores of these maladies had long since been discussed to distraction within the family. Prescription medicine bottles line cupboard shelves. They attest to her much doctoring over these many years. But then, Mom had been one of those early ones to be subjected to a radical hysterectomy – all those hormone producing and hormone regulating mechanisms scooped out of her in that 1940s operating room in that Mid-Western General Hospital.

What can't be disputed is timing. It was just about this time in her life – the time when things seemed to be converging and taking a noticeable down-turn that her use of the color yellow emerged. Perhaps, looking back at things, this color choice could be deduced to be a form of folk-therapy, self-administered. You know, surround yourself with what lifts the spirits and brings comfort – pretty practical, actually.

But by now, encroaching signs of dementia began to overshadow her depression of years earlier – those years throughout which she had struggled to maintain the high professionalism for which she was known and wondrously honored. Mom was seventy-five years old when the District School Board acknowledged her years of service, and finally, as Mom would chuckle, *allowed* her to retire from her long-time teaching position. She'd always been a staunch member of her mid-western community.

And now, I hear the water gurgling and splashing into the tub, "Come, Hillary," she's calling. "I need you to give me a hand."

I had not seen my mother during her advanced years – I mean, seen her in this kind of entirety. She was one to clothe herself discretely, professionally. In a strange way I felt touched to be summoned into her presence in this manner, and so matter-of-factly at that.

Consistent with the lemony yellowness of our surroundings, I made a point to be upbeat, bright, and also made a point to cast my eyes anywhere but on her bare, 90-some year old body.

But, of course, there *is* peripheral vision, and by it I take note of Mom's increasing shapelessness. Her skin, grown soft, almost too soft. In her later years, it disturbed me that Mom took a strangely fierce stance against physical exercise. I'd try to concoct games to play with her that would get her to move, to become active, but the moment I was no longer taking the lead, she would revert to her inert self.

"Here, please put your arm under my shoulder," she summons me as she tries several times to lift her leg up over the side of the bathtub.

"Maybe if you'll stand right here beside me . . . ," she suggests, and sure enough, she proceeds to let herself down ever so slowly into the tub. Once in the water, she begins to splash in earnest, up over her neck and shoulders, producing a scene of insurmountable contentment – a childlike joy.

"It's all right now, Dear. I'm fine." she says to me and gestures for me to relinquish my post and get about my out-of-the-bathroom business. "I'll call you if I need you. I just want to relax here, to be alone for a while."

But exactly what she meant by *alone* and *for a while* begins to unnerve me when, after a half hour passes, I have heard nothing. "How are you doing in there," I call, and I tap lightly on the bathroom door. "I thought you were going to call me."

"Well I didn't want to bother you, Hillary. I thought I could handle this on my own, but, well, come on in will you please, Dear? Maybe you can help me figure things out."

When I enter the bathroom, there is Mom still sitting in the bathtub exactly as I had left her, but she is far from contented. Mom had, earlier on, begun to show signs of mental confusion.

By now, the water temperature is tepid. She had let the water out of the tub, down to only an inch or so around her legs. Mom is cold. She's shivering slightly.

I grab a towel and put it around her shoulders, fully intending to help her out of the tub just as I had helped her into it. Together, we heave. We pull. We try every configuration we can think of to help her maneuver her feet under her in order to ease her into a standing position.

Nothing works.

With all this exertion, I happen to glance at my wristwatch. Is it playing tricks on me? By the watch hands, I note that we've been at this nearly an hour. I wrap more towels around Mom's shoulders. Then we try all over again. But still, Mom is not able to get her body into a position that will result in allowing her to stand up and step over the side of the tub and out.

Mom's skin has long since gone crinkly. Her lips are fast turning an unsettling grey blue.

As calmly as I can, I excuse myself and run to the phone but of course there is no way to track down my brother who, I was sure, could, with a single gesture, hoist mother up and out of that tub.

'Such a silly thing to do,' I scolded myself. 'Hadn't I blown off all possibility of being in contact with him when I so grandly told him to have a great time out with his family and not give us a single thought our evening? And the mere idea of dialing 911 was out of the question. By the time the village Fire Department crew would arrive, together with photographers and reporters from the *Village Gazette*, the whole thing would be out of hand. 'I'll be in charge, I'd boasted to my brother. So, I'm holding to that.'

I return to my mother who is still sitting in the same position in that tub. The time was now edging on toward two hours.

I'm at a loss to come up with any workable plan. Already I'd done what I could do to turn that yellow tub into a bed of sorts – at least until my brother arrives home. By this time, my silly confidence is mocking me, my watch hands, running ahead at top speed.

For a considerable time now the water has been completely out of the tub. I take this opportunity to leave Mom for a moment and I go to each of the bedroom closets for still more blankets and pillows to soften the hard ceramic tub surface when – distantly – I hear water running.

Fearful, I run back to the bathroom. There, amazingly, with the towels and blankets heaped on the floor to the side of the tub, the water turned on full force, is Mom – sitting erect, her demeanor, commanding. She is no longer the shivering, perplexed little lady in her nineties. In that brief amount of time, Mom had returned to become the clear thinker I had known her to be years before, the science teacher of enviable ability before dementia had assaulted and robbed her of so much of her mental acuity.

Commandingly, decisively, Mom is sitting there in the tub in all her natural glory, cranking the tub faucet – forcing the warm water to rise high around her.

Mother looks me straight in the eye and says, "Physics says to use all the best resources at hand. So in order for me to get out of here, I've got to bring together what the buoyancy of the water can offer, together with my body's ability to put it all to my best use."

Suddenly I'm even more unsure of things. I stand there, incredulous, watching as the water runs full force into that yellow ceramic bathtub – higher and higher – and as it does, Mom, holding on to both sides of the tub, begins to rock side to side, an expression of triumph on her face.

"Now this is the plan, this is what I'm going to do," Mom explains with mind boggling clarity, "I am going to allow the water to help me. When it gets to just the right height, my body's displacement will buoy me up. Then I'll roll over and I'll put my knees down first, then again, the water will raise me up just enough to slip my feet under me one at a time. Hillery, you stand right here to give me stability. You're going to see how the very water that threatened me is now going to help me."

I watch, my every muscle taut and at the ready to try to catch Mom if her plan fails. But instead, just as she calculated, the full tub of warm water elevates her entire body off the tub bottom. Up, she bobs.

Then, sure enough, over she rolls and in an instant she is on her knees. She grips my arm for support. First her one foot plants itself on the tub bottom, then the other. "Now turn off the water," she directs, "and open the drain – fast!" And with that, out whooshes the water down the drain, leaving Mom standing upright in the tub. She then takes my arm, steps up – one leg at a time – and out of that tub just as she had stepped into it hours earlier.

"Hey, you guys in here . . . ?" My brother has returned from his evening out. He pops his head in the bathroom door, peering at us through the steam. "You still in here . . . Talk about a spa night!" he teases, but then he notices all the blankets and pillows on the bathroom floor. He turns serious, "What's been going on?"

"Fun." Mother replies with the hint of a wink, as she pulls her towel tightly around her. "Nothing but fun the entire time you've been out." And she makes her way past us both – her head high – and on to her room.

A little later, I check on Mom. She's standing in the middle of her bedroom, a piece of clothing in each hand. There's a puzzled look on her face. I notice that spark, the light that had illuminated and animated my mother only moments before, has so very sadly gone dim once more.

Educator and freelance writer.

"The secret of genius is to carry the spirit of the child into old age, which means never losing your enthusiasm."
Aldous Huxley

NEVER SURRENDER

Donald Shephard

In 1935, with three million Britons unemployed during the Depression, Minnie Slaven, age 16, takes a six hour train journey to London and finds steady employment with Unilever where she meets and marries a fellow clerk.

Minnie marvels at her second story flat above their sister-in-law's in Loughton, twenty miles northeast of London. Two bedrooms means one for the wee bairns. Should the baby she is carrying be a boy, Minnie has a good Scottish name ready. Minnie works until her condition becomes apparent. After six months as a homebody, she delivers Ann. Frank's quick temper flares over what he calls frivolous expenses and what Minnie calls clothes for Ann. They argue over his motorcycle costs. Silence fills their evenings after spats until Minnie humors Frank so they rarely go to bed angry.

Pregnant again within eighteen months, Minnie wishes for a boy, but Dr. Bell never allows her to see her stillborn son. After the doctor leaves, Minnie persuades the midwife to allow her to hold the corpse. She sheds no tears. A year later, after patting her tummy and whispering her boy's name for nine months, Elizabeth arrives. For the second time, Minnie smiles at a newborn daughter, regretting she has no son. A year later, her fourth delivery tests her resolve. Summoned from his whiskey sopping on the fireside perch of the Holly Bush pub, Dr. Bell plops the stillborn boy into a bucket. Dr. Bell clamps his hands around Minnie's face and slurs, "It's obvious, you cannot bear boys."

"Never you mind the doctor, my dear, he's only a man," the attending midwife comforts her.

"That daft old sot scares me not a whit," the stalwart Minnie retorts. Rocking her baby, Minnie nods toward the door, "I've dodged rent collector thugs in Glasgow when my father left me with no money; I've traveled alone to London and made a living; and born two children from four pregnancies."

"Well said lass." The midwife scratches a mole on her nose and chuckles.

After Hitler invades Poland in September, 1939, the Royal Army calls Minnie's thirty-three year old husband, Frank, into His Majesty's Service. Food rationing begins early in the New Year. Whenever her sister-in-law complains of these irksome restrictions, Minnie says, "Duck soup."

She visits Frank in a Salisbury Plain army camp and conceives in the middle of February, 1940. Because of her history of stillborn sons, Dr. Bell assigns his most experienced midwife, who gives Minnie a National Health Service pamphlet depicting each stage of fetal development. Minnie loves the photo of the healthy baby boy, picturing herself nursing her Scottish named son. Marking off days on a calendar, she imagines her wee bairn growing in her womb. In her next letter to Frank she writes, "Your baby's rudimentary nervous system, brain, digestive system, ears and arms have already formed." He replies with a description of the street boys, who scavenge the rubbish dump outside the British Army compound.

At the beginning of March, Dr. Bell hears the fetal heart beat for the first time. In her weekly letter to Frank before the middle of the month, Minnie reports their baby has vestigial nostrils, eyelids, and nose. At the beginning of April, she tells him its fingers, legs, feet, toes, and bones have differentiated. The cardiovascular system functions fully, although the fetus measures less than one inch long. All this Minnie reads and reports to Frank with a pressing sense of wonder willing her baby to be a boy and live. Frank replies with a description of (*here the censor has blacked out a name*), an Arab urchin he has befriended.In April, 1940, Germany invades Denmark and Norway. Denmark surrenders immediately, but the Norwegians fight on with British and French assistance. The local council installs an Anderson shelter for Minnie. For this, men hand-dig a pit the size of a family grave plot in the orange clay behind her flat and bury a corrugated iron shelter with four bunk beds, two up and two down. They install a metal door and build steps down to it. After their eleven o'clock tea break, they cover and camouflage the iron with earth and sod. Minnie plants pansies atop the Anderson shelter in the concentric circles of blue, white, and red, the Royal Air Force emblem.

While the fetal torso lengthens to about one-and-a-half inches, Minnie pushes pins into a map to trace the progress of the war each time the BBC broadcasts allied and enemy lines retreating toward England. She studies the drawings in the midwife's pamphlet and pictures her baby's chin and face forming remarkably like her husband's, but with a dominant head.

In May, Minnie's fetus develops the practice of blinking its eyes and sucking its lips, and Germany invades Belgium, Luxembourg, and the Netherlands. Neville Chamberlain resigns, and Winston Churchill forms a coalition government. The fetal body outgrows the head, and Minnie feels activity in her baby's muscles, although it has only reached five-and-a-half inches long. If she stops to think, the combined discomforts and stresses of motherhood, war and pregnancy, worry her. She does not dwell on it.

The Netherlands and Belgium surrender to Germany. On the thirteenth of the month, Minnie listens to Churchill's "Blood, Toil, Tears and Sweat" speech. No doubt her unborn child can hear the oration and no doubt without understanding. She is not convinced it will survive both birth and World War II, and also learn to read Churchill's words. Later in May, Minnie listens to BBC reports about Operation Dynamo on her in-laws' accumulator-powered wireless. By June, when the disaster ends, the Royal Navy and a flotilla of privately owned small boats rescue 350,000 British, French and Belgian troops from Dunkirk. They leave all their hardware behind. Germans capture over a million Allied prisoners at a cost of 60,000 casualties in three weeks. Churchill warns, "Wars are not won by evacuations," and describes Dunkirk as, "a colossal military disaster." These words ring in Minnie's ears as she reads her daughters' bedtime story. Alone in her room, she listens to the end of Churchill's radio oration. "We shall defend our island whatever the cost may be. We shall fight on the beaches, we shall fight on the landing grounds, we shall fight in the fields and in the streets; we shall fight in the hills. We shall never surrender." Immune to Churchill's morale boosting, Minnie succumbs to sadness for the utter chaos of life and she allows herself to weep.

Sitting alone in her flat behind velvet blackout curtains, Minnie frets about her choices. If she bears another daughter, she'll have three to shepherd into the Anderson shelter. If the baby she carries is a boy, she faces several more months of discomfort climaxed with agony, resulting in another stillborn.

So, Minnie fills two suitcases with clothes and slams herself off her bed. Her ankles ache; pain racks the small of her back, otherwise—nothing. She grinds her teeth, climbs on the bed and jumps again. Shock forces her to drop the suitcases and sit on the bed. Her abdomen remains unfazed. "Well baby," Minnie says aloud, "if you are that determined to hang on, you may as well live."

The day after Churchill's broadcast, air raid sirens wail. Minnie hurries her two daughters underground where she tucks them into bed and tells them a story about kelpies, hearth fairies from her own childhood. Once they fall asleep, she reads about her baby's current state by the light of a candle, which wavers after each explosion. Fetal limbs achieve their final proportions; eyelashes and eyebrows appear and the new being has grown to six-and-a-half inches. Her in-laws have brought up Frank in the high Church of England, and he professes strong belief in its dogma. Minnie, raised Catholic, never goes to mass, never prays, so when she writes to her husband, about their baby-to-be, she omits the suitcase episode. Italy declares war on the United Kingdom on June tenth, and four days later, the Germans enter Paris. By changing his wife's initials on five successive envelopes home, Frank has signaled his assignment to Alexandria. Minnie replies that their baby by now has grown substantially in weight; its red skin has wrinkles and it measures thirteen inches.

The Luftwaffe launches the Battle of Britain in July, confining Minnie and her girls to subterranean life. The beech, hornbeam and oak trees of Epping Forest beckon her. After ten days cooped up in her flat, she treats her family to a picnic. Little Ann and Elizabeth skip happily along the leaf-strewn forest paths. A dogfight between a Royal Air Force Spitfire and a Luftwaffe Messerschmitt interrupts their giggling. Minnie calls to her daughters and grasps their hands as they watch the planes twist and spin above. Machines roar closer; she hustles her family into the bunker. Engines scream overhead as she clutches her brood. When she hears the distant all-clear siren, Minnie emerges only to learn that the Spitfire crashed into a wooded hill killing the twenty year-old pilot—another mother's son. *Would her boy survive all this only to die in war?*

Daily newspapers inform Minnie about the epic air battle that lasted until September and resulted in the indefinite postponement of Operation Sea Lion, the German plan to invade England. Frustrated by losses in the Battle of Britain, Hitler attempts to crush the British people by ordering the London Blitz. Nausea rises to Minnie's throat when the BBC reports this massive bombing of civilians has killed 43,000 and injured 140,000 more. German explosions damage or destroy a million cockney homes. Minnie and her girls escape to the underground shelter.

Newspapers trumpet Roosevelt's Lend-Lease program, giving Britain fifty much-needed destroyers. Late in September, Germany, Italy, and Japan agree to the Tripartite Pact. During the long nights of the blitz, Minnie writes to her husband, "Our baby's fingernails and toenails have sprouted and it has lengthened to fourteen-and-a-half inches." Frank responds with the life and times of (*here a censor had blacked out a name again*) another street urchin. When Minnie hints to her mother-in-law about Frank's interest in boys, she receives only a dismissive scowl.

Her radio informs Minnie that, although air raids continue over London and the southeast of England into October, Germany is losing bombers faster than they can repair or replace them. The BBC warns that nighttime raids would increase. On November 15th, Germany destroys much of Coventry's city center. Four days later, since all hospitals bulged with wounded servicemen, Dr. Bell orders Minnie to move closer to the shelter in case of an air raid. The midwife arranges for her to give birth in her sister-in-law's ground floor flat.

Despite Dr. Bell's prediction, young Fergus enters World War II oblivious to the carnage around him and his mother. Minnie smiles at her newborn in disbelief. The evening of his birth, she once again hustles her family underground. She carries her baby, holds onto Elizabeth's hand, and herds Ann down concrete stairs. Stepping gingerly in the dark, they descend into the buried corrugated shelter. This routine allows for no disobedience and welds strong bonds between mother and children.

In 1941, while Fergus suckled at his mother's breast, she listened to Churchill say, "Never, never, never give up." Minnie remembered the time she jumped off the bed. She had almost given up. Fergus had not.

Donald Shephard is a retired trainer with California EPA. He has written two novels, one hundred short stories and fifty poems. This is his first published work. He lives with his wife in idyllic Mendocino, California.

RANT

Annie Jacobs

I don't want to write.
I don't want to write a thing.
Or hear that what I wrote needs fixing.
I don't want to clean the house.
I don't want to watch what I eat.
I don't want to listen to my friends kvetching,
Or feel the sharp prick of their criticism,
However accurate.
I want my dishes to wash themselves;
My car to always stay clean.
I want to find every valuable thing I ever lost,
Including people and pets.

I want everyone who ever knew me
To remember me fondly.
And speak of what a wonderful person I am,
Even when I'm not.
I want a do-over for every wrong choice made
And every misspoken word uttered,
With clear cut directions on how to make

Everything turn out just right.
I want to be young and desirable again
And have Hot Sex with
Beautiful young men
All through the long nights of my
Resurrected youth.

Now really, is that too much to ask?

Annie Jacobs resides in Brooklyn, New York with her husband of 40 years and two dogs and one cat. She has been writing for many years; coming from a family of poets and writers. Re-writes are not her favorite thing.

PART 4

The Gift of Endless Benefits

"Wrinkles should merely indicate where smiles have been."
Mark Twain

A SHINY STICK OF LOVE

Maril Crabtree

When I came home from school, I saw the letter from Mammaw on the dining room table. It was addressed to me.

I picked it up and felt the telltale bulge. I ripped it open and a shiny stick of foil-wrapped chewing gum slid into my eager hands. At seven, I had no money to buy gum, and Mom never bought any at the store. This was my special treat from my grandmother. She wrote me once a month and never failed to put in a stick of gum.

Dear Granddautter, the letter said. *Hope you are haveing a good time at school. Dont forget to take the gum out when you go to class, or the teecher will get madd at you.*

Mammaw had a third grade education and spelling was not her strong suit. But I loved receiving her letters – and the gum. Sometimes there'd even be a dime taped to the flowered stationery she always used.

You can by a hole pack of gum with this, the letter would say.

Grandmother's letters continued all the way through grade school, except in the summers when Mom and Dad drove me to rural Arkansas and left me for three heavenly weeks in the tiny wood frame house Mammaw and Pappaw shared. Its three small rooms were stacked one behind the other. The kitchen sink had a pump for running water. An outhouse was the only bathroom and I slept on a cot in one corner of the kitchen where all the good smells came from: fresh biscuits and peach preserves, berry cobblers and apple pies.

Summers were my special time to be with Mammaw. She planted a huge vegetable garden, raised chickens, and spent the long daylight hours working outdoors. As a city kid, I delighted in working side by side with her.

It was my job to draw bucket after bucket of well water for baths and chores. I fed the chickens and hoed the corn, picked green beans and tomatoes, and stepped warily around the woodpile, watching for snakes. Once when we came out of the hen house we saw a huge black king snake slithering toward us. Calmly, Mammaw handed the egg basket to me and reached for the hoe. I watched, fascinated. With one quick motion, she swung the hoe and chopped off the snake's head.

"Weren't you scared it'd bite you?" I asked, safe on the back porch where I'd retreated.

"Heavens, no," she chuckled. "It knows I'd bite back!"

Every day with Mammaw held adventure and accomplishment. I watched her swing a chicken up by its feet with one hand, and with the other grab the slender neck. With a swift motion, she twisted the neck between her thumb and index finger, then jerked upward. I heard a distinct snap. Other than that, the chicken never made a sound.

"That's the best way to kill a chicken," she said. "It's a quick way, not as messy as chopping off its head with an axe."

For a while the chicken flopped this way and that around the back yard in a crazy figure eight, its head dangling. Finally, after it stopped flapping its wings, Grandmother scooped it up, brought it into the kitchen, and dipped it into a big pot of boiling water. "This will loosen the feathers," she said. Then she tied a bibbed apron around my waist, both of us chewing spearmint gum, and we set to work. With grandmother standing at the sink and me sitting on a stool beside her, we began to pluck feathers from the carcass.

"Don't take too many at a time," she cautioned me. "You don't want to tear the skin."

She showed me how to pull the feathers out and away from the body. Handful by handful, we plucked and picked. Mammaw's hands worked twice as fast as mine, but she waited patiently while I "helped." The stinky smell of wet feathers invaded my nostrils but I forced myself to think about the delicious fried chicken I knew we'd have for supper that night.

Then on hot July mornings she'd send me into the woods with a tin bucket.

"Go pick me some huckleberries, and I'll make us a cobbler for dessert tonight," she'd say.

She didn't have to say it twice. I dove into the thick green undergrowth and started picking. A couple of hours later, my bucket, brimming with shiny black berries and my body sweaty and itching with insect bites, I was ready to stand under the hose and take a cold outdoor shower, dreaming of how good that cobbler would taste.

As I grew older, vacations with Mammaw came less often. My summers filled with jobs as a camp counselor. Still, her letters came faithfully.

Well, its so hot today you cud fry an egg on a rooster's tail, so thot Id come inside & rite you this letter.

The shiny stick of gum was always there, and occasionally a quarter would be taped to the letter. For birthdays and Christmas, her letters always held a wrinkled dollar bill – and that juicy stick of gum.

I left home to attend a Midwestern university. All through college, every few weeks, she sent me letters, each one with a stick of gum. I'd long since stopped chewing it, but I still loved unwrapping the shiny foil, inhaling its distinctive smell and remembering all the times I sat next to her on the porch while we snapped beans and gum both at the same time.

Now dont go & marry one of those Kansas wheat farmers! she wrote. But when, after two years of college, I did get married, she wrote: *He seems like a nice man but hope the 2 of you stay in school until you finnish.* Then her letters contained two sticks of gum.

After Jim and I started our family, Mammaw's letters came less frequently. By then Pappaw had died and she moved into a small apartment in Memphis. Since she never learned to drive, the only time she got to the store was once a week when a friend took her. But on every birthday – mine, Jim's or the kids' – her cards still came, each with a dollar bill then and a stick of gum.

Mammaw is gone now. I often think of how much I learned during those summer sojourns: how to stop the pain of a bee sting with wet tobacco, how to ease eggs from beneath a protective hen, how to roll out biscuit dough and cut it into circles with a flour-edged drinking glass, how to wake up early bursting with eagerness to see what the day might bring.

Most of all, I learned how little it takes to make someone feel loved, as little as one shiny, foil-wrapped stick of gum. As my own grandchildren came along, I tried to make sure they felt special and loved. Several times a year they received a card with a handwritten note, and I often tucked something special into it – a packet of Pokémon cards or a gift card for their favorite treat. I hope they'll remember me someday as fondly as I remember Mammaw.

Maril Crabtree grew up in the South but calls the Midwest home. Her work appears in anthologies and journals such as *Persimmon Tree*, *Chicken Soup for the Soul* and *Steam Ticket*. She has two chapbook: *Dancing with Elvis* and *Moving On*, with a third, *Tying the Light*, forthcoming in 2014.

A CIRCLE OF CRONES

Elayne Clift

There are among us one uterus, three ovaries, multiple husbands, numerous children, several grandchildren, and six interesting careers. Two of us are cancer survivors. Another has a chronic disease. One has been sexually abused. We know better than most that Bette Davis was right: Old age is no place for sissies.

That is why we proudly call ourselves Crones – wise women of a certain age who are transitioning into the third stage of our lives with grace, spirited intelligence, humor and a sense of belonging in this world. We are no longer what Simone de Beauvoir called "the Other" nor do we suffer Betty Friedan's "problem that has no name." Rather, we live at the center of our lives, not because we wear red hats or sport large egos, but because we understand the gifts that have been granted to us, and because we cherish the centrality of connection to each other, and to the larger world, as we travel the life span.

Most people think of crones as haggard, shriveled, witch-like women who have nothing to offer but negative energy. Nothing could be farther from the truth. In pre-Christian, pre-patriarchal times, post-menopausal women were revered for their intellectual and spiritual gifts. Their counsel was sought by others because they were Wise Women. As healers and leaders, they were called upon at every occasion from birth to death, and they exercised the benevolent power of the ancient tribal matriarch.

Another way to think about Crones is that we are archetypes. Along with Maidens and Mothers, we represent a universal type of persona or character that transcends time and culture. We are the third archetype in the life cycle of females. While Maidens represent young, pure, idealistic feminine youth, and Mothers signify energetic females in their nurturing, most productive years, Crones symbolize wise older women whose knowledge of life is trusted and respected.

I came to know more about this, and the three stages of a woman's life, just as I was creeping up to my 50th birthday in 1993 and wondering how I would mark that significant event. Excited by what I had discovered, I decided to have a Croning Celebration for my own passage past that milestone. I wanted to share with special women friends I'd known through the important phases of my life, even though so many others seemed to dread this particular time. I didn't want to do anything bizarrely New Age; like howl at the moon. I just wanted to have a good time with a great group of women with whom I had shared significant stages of my life.

And so, on a windy weekend in March, full of the promise of spring, six women and I headed for the Eastern shore of Maryland. Our plan was to spend three days sharing, laughing, eating, drinking, walking, networking, and laughing some more. And as we expected, we've been Croning together ever since. Soon we will celebrate our 20th anniversary (and our

70th birthdays). We shared secrets, played hooky, went to Friday night movies and made endless fun of our teachers.

Our weekend at a condo in Rock Hall, Maryland, we talked about how we become friends over the travails of marriage and motherhood.

Lunch was followed by copious goods from Victoria's Secret. And my favorite present was a huge pin that said, "Don't You Wish You Looked This Good at 50?" It was the perfect accessory to the T-shirt that read "Wild Thing!" There were lots of cards and a poem that made me cry, and a steady flow of Chardonnay.

Later, after a long walk and a lot of connecting, we headed for dinner at a local seafood joint, escorted by Rock Hall's only cop. "Follow me!" he commanded, red light flashing which only added to the hilarity of it all. The restaurant was full of hearty, freckled fishermen who gawked at our entourage as if they'd never seen a gang of Crones before.

By the end of that wonderful weekend, our feast of friendship, shared female strength, pathos and humor – was deeply embedded in our collective psyche. We had shared so much, including boundless wit, plus the wisdom of that comes with age, occasional tears, a few extra pounds, abundant creativity, adventurous spirits and the great joy in our femaleness that knows we are bonded forever.

We've been meeting now at least three times annually in venues as diverse as the Caribbean, the Canadian Rockies, and the Colorado River for a rafting trip in the Grand Canyon. Sometimes we just hang out at each other's houses. Once my husband said, "But what do you *do* when you are together all that time?" Well, like I've said, we talk, laugh, eat, walk, explore, share and support each other. We celebrate milestone birthdays and new romances. We counsel each other about the challenges we continue to face as parents and partners. We have consoled the one among us who became widowed and the two of us who've been ill.

When we are apart, we email regularly with jokes, advice, book or movie recommendations, and one-line rejoinders. We have developed our own lexicon, which includes such terms as Crone Mobile (a van), Crone crotch (the loss of pubic hair as one ages), and Crone cry (a plea for help). We are planning to have a Crone Cottage when we are all elderly (ideally staffed by a nurse, a cook, and a toy boy). We take turns organizing our Croning trips, which take us farther and farther afield these days.

One of the beautiful things about "The Crones" is that all our other friends know about us. Some of them ask to be included in the next Croning when our gatherings are local. Others have started their own Crone groups. We love having spawned similar gangs of women, like an overactive spider plant that keeps sprouting healthy new offshoots. Our daughters have talked about emulating us with their chums when their Croning time comes.

Nearly twenty years have gone by and we still have more fun together than any other group of friends I've ever known. And we are absolutely there for each other, closing ranks, no matter what kind of support is required. These women are my sisters and my soul mates, my chosen family. Individually and together, we understand the beauty and the necessity of female friendship and solidarity. We know that each of us is larger in life than we would be without each other and that without any one of us, we would all be diminished. We are mindful of its responsibilities, and we cherish its rewards. Because we have each other, we are centered. We feel balanced. We are whole.

Elayne Clift is an award-winning writer, lecturer and workshop leader. U.S correspondent for the India-based Women's Feature Service, columnist for the *Keene* (NH) *Sentinel*, and reviewer for The New York Journal of Books, her latest book and first novel, *Hester's Daughters*, appeared in 2012. She lives in Saxtons River, VT. www.elayneclift.com

BENT – NOT BROKEN

Cherise Wyneken

Ethel puts her hands on the arms of the chair and pushes down as hard as she can, trying to raise herself to answer the phone. After the third try, she makes it. "Hold on," she calls out, feeling her way to the desk.

"Hi, Grammie," comes the familiar voice. "This is Becky, calling about Christmas. The gang will all be here, and that means you too. Jack will come to get you. Plan on staying over and spending Christmas day with us."

"Stay over?" But what about Spunky? I know you don't like dogs."

"Ask your neighbor to look after him. It's just one night. You can't spend Christmas alone."

And so it was arranged. Arranged – like most things seemed to be now. Ethel had been fighting the battle for independence ever since she was pronounced legally blind. She had hoped to remain in her little yellow house at the end of Mulberry Lane for the rest of her life. Having gone from normal vision to macular degeneration, the small black speck in the center of her eye was slowly growing and affecting her peripheral vision as well, making daily living harder. Each year brought further complications. From cataracts to operations, from thick eyeglass lenses to a white tipped cane. From keeping house and crocheting afghans to hiring housekeepers and watching the evening news not with her eyes but with her ears.

Helpful suggestions from the local Blind Society – like how to manage the stove, connect the right shoe to the right foot, measure liquid being poured into a glass, locate utensils at the table, and how to use her cane, along with help from relatives and friends, had extended her independent living. Now eighty-seven and arthritic, she finds herself struggling to win the fight.

"Come live with us," her son had urged from Southern California"

"They have wonderful retirement places now, her daughter said. "Why not move to one of them?"

To every suggestion, Ethel had an excuse; and especially, "What would I do with Spunky?" As she packed her overnight bag she began to wonder, 'Am I doing right by staying on my own? Like right now – with Jack having to come all the way over here to pick me up. I'm becoming more and more dependent on others. Is it fair to them? Everyone doing for me while I do nothing for others?'

Admittedly, frustrations were multiplying. Well-meaning people who straightened out her things leave her unable to find what she's looking for. It's becoming more difficult to discern which pills are in which bottles. Her clothes collect spots she is unable to see until her daughter comes from out-of-state and cleans them. Her hand must now be guided to the line for her to sign her checks, and she can only wonder if there are ants on the kitchen counter where she spilled the orange juice.

But this is Christmas, she reminds herself. So she puts aside her problems and gets ready for Jack.

After warm greetings and helpful hands guiding her down the stairs, they lead her to a corner of the living room to a large, soft chair. Although her back is to the view of the San Francisco Bay, the sun shines down and warms her.

As the others drift off to do their chores or to play, Ethel realizes she feels more alone than when she is by herself at home. At least, she thinks to herself, I have Spunky there. And I'll miss going to church for the Christmas service.

At last, she hears footsteps approaching, and the clink of ice.

"Here, Grammie. How about a bit of Christmas cheer?"

Then the doorbell rings. More greetings. More footsteps on the stairs. She sees each family member enter – her eyes fastened to her ears.

"Who is standing near me? Move a little to my side so I can see your face."

After hugs all around, Ethel stretches out her hands, searching. "Someone's missing," she says. "Where's that handsome husband of yours, Trish?"

Ethel's question is met with silence. Then someone clears her throat. "They're not together anymore," Debbie says. "Trish kicked him out."

"Kicked him out? But why? I thought you two were so in love."

Trish takes Ethel's glass. "Things happen, Grammie. Let me get you a refill."

Once again everyone drifts off: Becky and Debbie to the kitchen – chatting, preparing food. The kids to the den to play

Nintendo. Nat to the piano with Phyllis nearby on her flute – playing Christmas music. Cold creeps in around her neck and down her arms along with the setting sun and whiffs of roasting quail. Ethel tries to hum along until she hears footsteps once again and she finds Trish returning with her refill.

"Thank you, Dear," Ethel says. "Now sit down a bit with me. Tell me all about it."

"Oh Grammie, I was afraid you'd ask. I'm too ashamed to tell."

"Well, do it anyway. It can't be all that bad."

"Oh, yes it is – Jimmy's been untrue to me. You know – with another woman."

Ethel reaches for Trish's hand and squeezes it warmly. "It's not the first time a man's done something like that."

"Well, it's the first time for me – and I hate it. He says he wants to make up and vows he'll never be untrue again. But Grammie, how can I ever trust him now?

"You have a point, Dear. But take him back – let him prove himself. It's what you must do. Even cops don't always press charges on a first offense. Then if he strays again, you'll know what you are dealing with and can take steps. There is no marriage without trust. But there must be a place for forgiveness, too."

"I can't do that, Grammie. It hurts too much."

Ethel moves Trish's hand up to her own cheek. "See this scar, Dear? You should have seen me when I fell . . . all red and oozing. It was hard for me to appear in public – it looked like I'd been beaten. But gradually the red turned to a scab. Then the scab came off. It left a fiery scar. Now you can barely see it. Your wound is still fresh. Give it time."

"That's not the same, Grammie. My wound is on the inside."

"Those kind heal, too. Your granddad was unfaithful once, too. But look at all the great times we had together as we healed. I really loved that man. I would have been very lonely without him."

Ethel lets go of Trish's hand and gives her a gentle shove. "Go on, Child. Call him. Tell him to come join us. What's Christmas without Jimmy and his bass viol?"

Later, after dinner is served and gifts exchanged, Jimmy comes and sits down beside Ethel.

"How can I ever thank you, Grammie? Trish says that she will talk."

Cherise Wyneken is a freelance writer whose prose and poetry have appeared in a variety of publications. Her books include: *Round Trip, Freddie, SpaceShip Lands in Africa, Stir-Fried Memories* (prose); *Touchstones, Seeded Puffs, Old Haunts, Things Behind Things* (poetry). Plus a children's cassette: *Space Mouse Learns to Pray*, published by permission of Haworth Press.

URGED TO ACTION

Jean M. Gardner

The ground shakes. Shock waves spread out for miles. As much as I strain, I can't see the source of the tremor, but I can see a distant fifty miles in the brilliant light above the desert floor.

My car shudders under me. Little tufts of clay rise like minispouts into the air before settling down again to their desert rest. No skyscrapers to obstruct my view of the enormous, unending sky, up here in Northern Arizona, the sky is closer than anywhere I have ever been.

My destination is a Hogan, a round dome made from cedar logs and clay, a typical home to the Navajo people who have occupied Black Mesa for many hundreds of years. Even up until 1985 they were still living the old way, speaking the *Dineh* language, living their religion close to the land. Most were sheepherders dependent for their life on the welfare of their flocks, which moved like rainless white thunderheads across the land.

"The rain falls because of the water underground," an old Indian told me. "The water underneath magnetizes the rain in the clouds. But now the mine is sucking up all the water causing a drought."

I know I am passing over the massive Colorado River Aquifer, the major water source for Phoenix, Las Vegas and Los Angeles some 500 miles away. But the Navajos who have lived here for centuries are now forced to truck in their water. I have heard of a proposed plan to relocate these 10,000 Navajo. I am here because I want to find out more. Why is it necessary to uproot the last of North America's traditional people who have managed to hang on out here in the middle of nowhere for at least 400 years?

"Relocation Kills" reads the sign on the door of the Navajo Legal Defense Office in Flagstaff where I had stopped for directions. The attorney is young, fresh out of law school, but what he lacks in experience he makes up with passion.

"Its' greed that's causing it," he says, "the Peabody Coal Mine is just north of Big Mountain where you're going." He gets up from his desk and stomps over to a map on the wall. Stabbing his finger on a spot in Northern Arizona, he spits out the words, "This mine is the biggest open-air coal mine in the world. The pollution is so bad the only thing spaceship Voyager could see in the earth's atmosphere was the smoke from their coal-fired power plant. They have already taken more coal than any mine on earth, but they still want more!" He lets out a deep sigh as he returns to his desk in disgust.

"I don't understand," I say, "Why are they uprooting the Navajo families?"

"The Navajo reservation is sitting on a lot of money," he sneers. "This land, Big Mountain, sits on black mesa. It was considered worthless when they put the Indians here. But since then it's found to contain billions of tons of coal. Still nobody here has electricity. Instead, this power is turning on the lights in Las Vegas and L.A. You know we need plenty of power for those slot machines."

I've seen the movies, I think to myself. Back then, Tribal Councils were like councils of old sitting around a fire discussing local issues, but now Tribal Councils are legal corporations under the Department of Interior, and both stand to gain some of the spoils. I've heard how the government divided the land with a fence, one half to the Navajo and one half to the Hopi. Divide and conquer being the objective.

I learned a lot more since my arrival a month ago to meet a group of volunteer activists with sentiments similar to my own. We rented a house in Flagstaff close to both the Navajo and Hopi reservations. We do whatever we can to publicize the relocation of the Navajo who have had to uproot themselves from the Hopi side. The American people have to be informed, I felt. At least the tragedy would not go unnoticed by the rest of the country.

After thanking the young attorney for his help, I continue my drive to the Hogan. I think back to the first day on the reservation when I arrived at the Survival Camp, just before dawn. A grandmother was there already awake. She had motioned to me to pick up the stacked kindling and follow her. She was going to light the morning fire in a sacred manner as all the grandmothers did every morning before dawn. As we walked she stooped over to pick up tiny little plants growing out of the red clay earth.

"This one is good for mothers after a baby is born," she said, "and this one is good for the stomach. But don't eat this one or you'll have a bad stomach alright!" and she laughed her little laugh.

The grandmother and her family were scared. Everything in their reality was about to become alien, a world hostile to Indians even now in the twentieth century. I had been there to meet the old Navajo grandmother, her two daughters and eleven children in that Hogan. The sole man of the family reluctantly worked at the very mine they all feared. But then, this was the only source of employment for 300 miles. The family only saw him when he came home on weekends.

I was aware that in the Navajo culture, a matriarchy, the grandmother is the source of strength and stability for her family. The welfare of the whole family is her responsibility. She rises at dawn to offer her prayers and light the sacred fire. She owns the sheep and the Hogan. She is the teacher of the songs, prayers sung all day long as she goes through the chores of the day. She follows the sacred *Beauty Way* all of her life. She'd sing:

>*Beauty before me, there I wander.*
>*Beauty behind me, there I wander.*
>*Beauty all around me, in old age traveling.*
>*Beauty all around me, there I wander.*

In their oral culture the grandmother holds the wisdom of the past and she's responsible for teaching the young. She's the one who passes on the language and history. In this case, she is a four foot, eleven inch *David* pitted against the *Goliath* of the Peabody Coal Mine.

"You white people don't realize that our Mother Earth is a living being," she had said. "We're her children and she nourishes us at her breast. This place where we live, here on Big Mountain, is the liver of the mother earth," the grandmother turned away sadly. And I thought of the pure Colorado River water filtering through the massive coal field underneath us like a gigantic charcoal water-filter.

Just then, a tremor jolts me from my reverie. The road turns to the left toward the sound and I turn with it. I drive down into a dry wash and then up, cresting at about fifty feet.

Then I see it, the undeniable source of the rumble. It is *Big Mo* – the biggest earth digging machine in the world. It stands out in silhouette against the bright desert sun. Slowly it raises its bucket into the air, swiftly slashing down, slicing into the earth with a vengeance. Over and over again, its jaw scoops up the land. It takes only a single scoop to fill the entire bed of a waiting thirty- ton dump truck, which then scurries out of the way for the next one in line. From where I am, the machinery looks like ants, yet there is a man standing next to the dump truck who doesn't even reach the hubcaps. This monster is seven stories high. Its bucket lifts thirty tons of coal in one scoop. There is *Big Mo* with five huge relatives on the site each doing its best to devour the earth as fast as it can. The crater left behind is a monstrous, black open wound which, in this fragile desert environment, can never be healed again.

"We call it a National Sacrifice Area," one of the Arizona Senators had told us when we activists went to his office in Washington. "The Navajos will have to go."

"Go where?" I had asked.

A simple question, but obviously loaded. We all knew they were planning to purchase land by the Rio Puerco River. "Well

... to the border towns .... and to the New Land*s*." His eyes dropped as I looked at him.

The attorney had told me earlier the so-called *New Lands* set aside for the Navajo's relocation were actually radioactive wastes. But the *New Lands* had been contaminated by the biggest nuclear accident in the nation. A holding dam, left behind by a departed uranium company, gave way and dumped tons of radioactive waste down the Rio Puerco River, the sole water source for the *New Lands*. The half-life of the contamination was thought to be 12,000 years, he had added.

Already I had seen what happened to Indians in the border towns – broke, desperate and drunk, with nothing to live for. No more sheep, no more wool, no more weaving. No more horses. No more gathering herbs for medicine.

My heart is heavy. Tears begin to flow as I head for the Hogan where the Navajo grandmother is waiting with her eleven grandchildren.

When I first made this trip, after hours of searching down the unmarked dirt roads, I found the grandmother standing outside her closed door, a rifle clutched across her chest.

"We ain't going," I remember her saying. "We ain't moving no matter who says to!" She squints, fixing me with a piercing eagle-eye. 'This is my home. It was my parent's home and my grandparent's home – all the way back to the beginning. She raises the gun higher, "My children's' umbilical cords are buried here. When I die, this is where they'll raise their kids. Now git, before I have to use this thing!" and she waves the old gun menacingly.

Behind her the wooden Hogan door is plastered with bumper stickers: R*elocation is Genocid*. *No more Trail of Tears. Repeal Public Law 93-531.*

The Hogan is made of red earth and looks like a little round dome, "the womb of the Mother," they call it. As I shift my gaze. I quickly take in the surroundings; the flat clay earth, the sparse vegetation, the cedar trees like living beings against the endless horizon.

The Hogan really fits this landscape, I had thought. It really is like a womb. Somehow it feels comforting.

A sheepskin hangs from a cedar branch, drying gray and dusty. Once, there had been many sheep. Now there are only a few animals since the government confiscated their flocks hoping to drive the Indians away. It hasn't been easy for the old ones since that time. The sheep are their main food source and provide wool they use to weave in the ancient way. Selling their rugs is their only source of cash. A corral stands with high walls, rough cedar logs stacked in a circle next to an old pick-up truck. Bits of rusting tin and plastic lay about. And I think to myself, white man's trash doesn't recycle like clay pots and reed baskets.

"We'll never relocate," she says. "We're like the badger. You can't git him out of his hole!" She laughs and, just for an instant, I see a mischievous little girl but I know she would use that gun if she had to.

"There is no word in Navajo for relocation," she had said. *"*For us, relocation means to disappear forever.*"*

I knew she had to truck her water in now that the wells had gone dry. It was getting dryer every day. That's when I'd learned that the coal mine was sucking up the precious water from the aquifer at the rate of three million gallons a day.

Much has happened since we first met.

The relocation crews have been putting up the three hundred mile fence. I notice the fence as I drive along the road as it stretches across the virgin land. There had never been a fence out here in sheep country before.

Just like a John Wayne movie. Now it would be fences that defined the land . . . and divide the people, the cynic in me thinks.

The Dineh have been nomads in the old days and the custom remains today as they move their sheep between their summer and winter camps. Their burials, shrines, and umbilical cords all tie them to the land of their ancestors. Historians say the Navajo came across the land bridge in the Bering Sea back in the ice age, but the Dineh say they emerged from under the ground through a hole in one of their four sacred mountains, a place that is revered to this day. They say the Great Spirit gave them instructions to take care of the land with their prayers. Since then they have lived in harmony with the mother earth, praying and living *The Beauty Way*, singing their songs all day long. They don't need a TV or a telephone. They seem content with a life full of hidden meanings that I can barely grasp.

"You see that old woman out there walking her sheep?" a young Navajo once said to me. "You think she has nothing. You feel sorry for her. But, she is happy. She has everything she wants."

As I approach the Hogan once again, I see the fence running right across the land in front of her home. It must be cutting her off from the watering hole, I think with despair.

She sees me and says, "It's getting hot."

The door closes, scooping in the last of the light. I find myself inside of the round dome. It is dark and cool.

"The Hogan is sacred," she had told me. "It's built in a sacred way and the door always faces the East."

The most dominant thing in the Hogan is a big loom sitting in the middle of the floor with a half woven rug suspended in bright colors hanging in the dim light. She tells me that she made the loom from odd bits and pieces of wood, an old bed, pieces of pipe and twine. She also raises sheep, shears the wool, picks herbs and roots to make dye, washes and cards the wool, spins the yarn and dyes it before she even begins to weave the rug. It takes months of hard work to complete. There is no sink, no running water, and no electricity. Later, at night, when the expanse of dark sky is brilliant with stars, I am grateful for the lack of lights, which would have spoiled the night.

"Let me take a look at you," the old woman says as she goes to a cupboard where she takes out a beautiful woven basket. "Here is my medicine bundle." She takes a wrapped deerskin out of the basket and unties the leather thongs. Taking a small jar from inside, she hands it to me saying, "Mix this clay with fat and smear it all over your face. Now I'll fix you some tea."

She peers into my face. I squirm under her gaze. I am keenly aware of my white, fair skin which is now swollen and bruised from the bites of little gnats that tend to nest in sheep's wool.

I wonder how come the Navajos never seem to get bitten? I hope I'm not getting blood poisoning. "They told me over at the Survival Camp that maybe you could help me."

The old woman is a medicine woman, I had been told. She heals people with plants. We are 300 miles from the nearest hospital over rough, rutted roads . . . no clinic, no pharmacy, no doctor. As I stand in front of the old woman, I feel my life is in her hands.

She boils water on the two-burner propane stove and she begins to speak. "All of our sacred songs and prayers are here within our four sacred mountains. The teachings of our ancestors are here in our songs and prayers and are part of our ceremonies. They are our teaching and way of life. The land is our religion. We are connected to the land. Here is where we make offerings to the Spirit Beings for hundreds of years. Here we are known by the Spirit Beings. If we went to the *New Lands* we would not be known."

She brings me a large cup and fills it with tea made from cedar buds. She sits down across the room. Even with her wrinkled face, she looks beautiful and strong. "This is our religion, our way of life. If you cut out a person's heart and take it away, the person will die. Our Creator places us here on this land. We are part of Mother Earth's heart."

I open the medicine jar and find that it contains red earth. In time, the clay mixture works and the swelling begins to go down.

"Oh thank you. I don't know if I could have survived without your help. Thank you so much for your healing and caring enough to help me." At that moment, I know I will love her forever.

The next day we meet again at the Sun Dance. I see her skipping around the huge dance arena like a young girl and I think, if the day ever comes when they come to take you away, I want to be there too, standing with you.

My heart swells as the drums begin to beat and the eagle-bone whistles begin to shrill in unison to the rhythm. I know then that I too am a Sun dancer. I have suffered for the people and I feel I am a protector of the earth too.

Today the old woman is still in her Hogan but her children and most of her neighbors are gone. The mine has been closed because the pollution degraded the air in the Grand Canyon, and because the sacred springs have gone dry. The Tribal Councils will no longer sign mining leases. Peabody Coal has been ordered to install scrubbers, a technology called "clean coal" but considered too expensive to use.

My work is finished. I have helped bring attention to a critical problem.

It had been Jane Fonda who urged me into action. There she was on TV, looking gorgeous in her mid-70s, urging women coming to the end of their lives to "be that feisty girl again."

"This is the last act," she'd said, "time for adding it all up. What would you say about yourself? What would your family say? This is the last call; make the most of it."

Jane had long been a hero of mine. Her daring visit to North Vietnam during the Vietnam War caused an uproar in society. I admired her courage to take on the system and be free. I'm one of those renegade women who emerged during the 1950s, who dared to forge ahead toward the truth of their being. Struggling with our role in the world, we turned what was called *a woman's place* upside down. Being a wife and mother, raising children and propagating the human race were all that was expected of us back then, and we were expected to be and act in a certain way. Not that these were not worthy goals, but somehow it just wasn't enough. I felt there had to be more. Therefore, throughout my life I've been actively seeking social justice.

I can still hear the grandmother's song ring in my ears, "Beauty before me, there I wander; beauty behind me, there I wander; beauty all around me, in old age traveling . . . There I wander . . ."

The author spent years supporting the Traditional Native American efforts to stop the Peabody Coal Mine from forcing relocation of 10,000 Navajo people from their reservation. In addition to writing documentary scripts, her stories have appeared in numerous small publications. She is currently at work on her memoir.

"The question is not whether we will die, but how we will live."
                                                         Joyce Borysenko

LET SOMEONE HOLD YOU

Paul Morrissey

"Nattie was the greatest person that ever lived! I would rather have been shot myself, have my arms cut off, anything! . . . if it could have saved her."

Tears rolled down his cheeks unashamedly onto her nightgown. I didn't know whether to laugh or scream at this claustrophobic drama.

Red-faced, Dominic suddenly turned toward me. "And, Father Paul, you tell that jerk, God, that he can go screw himself for such a wicked, damn . . ." he broke off, whimpering like a child. I began to shift uneasily, my feelings, or lack of them, laid bare by this outburst.

Dominic laid Natalie back down on the pillow and kissed her. He dropped his unshaven face down a few inches from Natalie's as though to get one last look at her. My embarrassment melted into pity.

"Baby, baby!" he slapped her lightly on the cheek, "give me a sign, will ya? Blink your eyes, please? Anything! Just show me you're okay! If anyone can make a deal with God, Nattie, you can?"

I smiled when he so accurately characterized his wife.

"Dominic," I leaned close to him, "would it be okay to read a Psalm?" I thought this might bring some closure.

"Okay, okay." It seemed to crash through to his normal self and pull him back momentarily to reality.

After the Psalm, Dominic asked that I stay with him in the room. Then without another word, and as though I were invisible, Dominic lay down on the king-size bed and rolled over next to his wife's body. Embracing her, he began to converse tenderly as though she were still alive. Intimate things bubbled up from his heart, endearments maybe never before expressed, or maybe never so clearly uttered all the months he clung to the hope she'd get better.

I felt as if I had stumbled upon a couple making love. At first, I wanted to escape, but taking a deep breath, I sat down on the bed by their feet. I tried to imagine the fiery ball that was Natalie's soul, and prayed silently that her lingering spirit could depart.

"I love you, Baby, I love you!" murmured Dominic. In my mind, a voice was reciting words from marriage vows at weddings I had conducted over the years, "I promise to love you both in good times and in bad times, whether for richer or poorer, whether in sickness or in health . . . ."

It seemed so bizarre at first, but when Dominic whispered "You'll always be my sweetheart, Nattie . . . I'll miss you so much," suddenly I felt very blessed to be witnessing this parting act of love between Dominic and his beloved Natalie.

When someone dies, the feelings cover a whole spectrum: guilt for having caused it or for being left alive when a loved one goes; or maybe anger at the person for leaving; even a secret relief that the person is finally at peace – and so are we, thank God.

In my work as a hospice chaplain, I've often noticed people grieving when they feel that they didn't do enough. Sometimes there's an instinct to blame someone for what seems so unjust – the doctor, a relative, God, even the lost loved one. These feelings emerge in their own time and hit us in waves. One feeling may predominate for a while, then at other times they are all mixed up together.

Stephen Levine, the author of *Who Dies? An Investigation of Conscious Living and Conscious Dying*, says that grief "tears open the human heart" in order that we may understand our true selves in a way much deeper than we have done up to then. Only when we lose those things that we have based our identity on, he explains, do we begin to get a glimpse of the "I AM" beneath these things, the One who will live on when "I" have died. This knowledge doesn't take away the pain or the grief until the process has run its course, but it can help us to bear with our own and others' grieving and trust that it is teaching us something profound.

"The Lord gave, and the Lord has taken away; blessed be the name of the Lord," I recited the poignant words from Job. After this, Dominic and I joined the others in the living room. He introduced me to Natalie's daughter, Rochelle, by a former marriage. A brunette in her early twenties, she had a striking figure like her mother's before her sickness. Rochelle's husband grasped my hand warmly and told me he appreciated me being there. An older man with a shock of white hair pulled me aside. This uncle recounted how close he had been to Natalie, noting sarcastically that one of her aunts had left less than a week ago for a Caribbean cruise. Also milling about the room were a crowd of Natalie's colleagues from the theater, bright-looking women and men who appeared devastated and hung together in small groups.

Dominic's sister came up and told me, "The undertaker's in the lobby. Will you keep my brother occupied at the bar?"

Dominic was chatting with Cindy from Long Island, who was bartending. She offered me a cocktail of grapefruit or cranberry juice with vodka when I sat down, but I declined.

A couple of actors placed a brocaded dividing screen between us and the vestibule. "Keep his back to the door," one of them whispered to me. I'll try, I thought, but felt panicky. What if Dominic turns around and sees them, even runs after the body with his emotional style?

"Changed my mind!" I motioned to Cindy with a grin. "I'll have one of those drinks after all."

"Go for it, Father Paul!" said Dominic.

I had gulped a third of it down when I noticed a commotion behind the screen. "These are good, Dominic . . . you sure you don't want one?"

With his wrecked face, Dominic stared at me. "Later . . . I'll get drunk later."

As they zipped up the remains of his wife into a body bag in the next room and hustled it out the door behind us, Dominic philosophized, "Can you believe it? . . . we come into life all pink and cuddly, and in the end they take us out like a pile of garbage!"

I gagged on my drink, laughing at his outrageous imagery. Cindy and he got napkins while I choked and fussed until the door closed.

Quickly, the screen came down and an air of relief settled over the room. Some lit up cigarettes. The group of young people piled next to each other on the long, white sofa. The talk became more animated and even included some soft laughter. At one point, Rochelle came over and whispered something in Dominic's ear and he nodded. Soon, long-stemmed glasses were being handed out to everyone and a bottle of champagne was poured. "Nattie's favorite," mumbled Dominic.

I wasn't sure what was happening but accepted a glass when it was offered. Everyone stood, including Dominic. With arms wrapped around each other, we lifted our glasses high in the air as Rochelle led us in a toast: "As Mom would say," she announced with a husky voice, 'Here's to those who wish us well, and all the rest can go to hell!'" Her slender arm shot straight up while applause erupted, including shouts of testimony to Natalie's vitality and love for life. We clicked our glasses and sipped. Yes, not to Death, their defiant faces taught me, not to Death do we drink, but to Life! L'Chaim!

Later that night before retiring, I went up to the fourth floor solarium in our rectory in the Bronx. I wanted to remember Natalie so I lit a candle in the dark. Dominic's words came to my ears, "Give me a sign, Baby!" The next moment a clap of thunder struck right above my head! This was followed by brilliant bursts of lightning. Over and over they crackled around me right outside the windows, lighting up the sky as though it were noonday.

I shook in my place then the thought came: It's Natalie's sign! When was the last time a storm with such ferocity hit New York? It felt as if it were Natalie's spirit taking off. Not easily would she go. "Baby, give me a sign that you're okay?" Dominic had pleaded. Yes, this lady would light up the sky with her life, even on the day she said goodbye.

So, you who read these tales of wit and wisdom, celebrate your life today. Thank God or Yahweh or Buddha or the Higher Power or your parents for this one inimitable life you have. Who else could bring your exquisite, if sometimes quirky, personality to the world? Look out through your eyes. Maybe they're a little dimmer now. Who cares? Let the world look back at you. What a life! Keep on living it to the hilt. No one can do it your way. You are perfectly imperfect and that is just enough.

Paul F. Morrissey is a Catholic priest and prison chaplain. He is the author of a memoir, *Let Someone Hold You: The Journey of a Hospice Priest*. (Crossroad, 1994). He is in the process of publishing a novel, *The Black Wall of Silence*.

I AM

Linda Mellen

I do not need to look for love
    I am love itself.
I do not need to wish for peace
    I am peace itself.
I do not need to run from suffering
    I am all the suffering in the universe.
I do not need to leap for joy
    I am all the joy in all the worlds.

I am the Source, and all the products of that source.
    I am the Beginning, and
    I am the End.

I am coming to your house.
I am no other than your larger Self, coming to comfort
    Your small, confused self.
Will you be waiting for me
    On your front porch
    Relaxed, ready, open?

Or will you be scurrying about inside your house
Preoccupied with the tangled thorns
of what you think of as your life:
Family, duties, work, the opinions of friends?
Will you be afraid of me?
Or will you walk quickly out to me, bravely,
        Rejecting all your past, all your future, in one second,
Greeting me *now*, smiling, arms open?

I am Love.
I have been with you always.
I have been waiting for you always.
I am your own Self, come to hold you once again,
        Never to let you go.

A beautiful and creative soul, Linda Mellen died in September, 2011.

TOUCHSTONES OF FAITH

Linda Berkery

For the past twenty-five years, whenever I have faced a difficult trial, or feel uneasiness in my faith, I return to the same "touchstone" memory. It was the day when a change of health taught me to cherish small moments, and write daily prayers of gratitude. It began with the day I focused on the present rather than fear of the future.

On a cold January day with a brilliant blue sky, I was roasting a turkey and frosting a cake for my husband's birthday. The baby was napping and four-year-old Tommy was upstairs with his new friend, Glenn. Lego sounds of clinking, dumping, and swishing blended with giggles. I remember checking the clock when the garage door opened. I was not expecting to see my husband Jack until dinner.

"Why are you home so early?" I asked. Jack mumbled, grabbed some Tylenol, and climbed upstairs. I quickly basted the turkey and followed him. I had known Jack since we were fifteen. He had never complained of headaches nor left work early, and though he was always a man of few words, mumbling was very unusual.

"Something is terribly wrong," I thought and I crawled under the covers with Jack. Stroking his head, I silently prayed for healing and understanding. I don't remember feeling panic or fear at the time – just a strong awareness that this was not a simple headache he was having. I didn't know what it was, but I felt it was significant.

Then Jack fell asleep and I went downstairs. I'd called little Glenn's mom, a nurse, and she offered to take the two children. "It's probably something ordinary – nothing to worry about," she said, hustling the boys into her old wagon.

Certainly for someone only thirty-nine, a stroke seemed out of the question.

That afternoon Nanny, Jack's mother, stopped by. I was really glad to see her since this day was rapidly becoming overwhelming. When Jack awoke, I became alarmed. He tried to speak but his nouns and verbs were jumbled. Syllables were out of order. And to add to the pressure, I could see that he was aware of his speech problems but still he refused an ambulance. So turkey and all the birthday fixings, along with the baby, were left in Nanny's care. I rushed Jack to the nearest hospital.

The ER doctor gently guided me through the process of admission. "You need a specialist, but I am not allowed to make a recommendation," he said. "However, if you were to tell me that you heard Dr. J was a wonderful physician, well then, I would most certainly agree," he nodded. I picked up his clues and requested the outstanding specialist. After many tests Jack was attached to a heart monitor and admitted for observation. Later, I drove home feeling very alone.

We thought there had been no warning of Jack's stroke until we remembered a brief comment by a pediatrician one time that his heart valve might cause problems around age forty due to a childhood case of rheumatic fever. But my husband was a runner in good physical shape. Just the previous Sunday, he had spent hours making and painting large "snow helmets" with the children to celebrate the Super Bowl. What we learned later was that the stroke occurred when a flick of scar tissue around the aortic valve traveled to the brain. Being strong and healthy made no difference in Jack's case.

When I arrived home from the hospital around midnight, I found the children asleep and my mother-in-law lying on the couch. After Nanny left, I went in to turn off the dining room light. I felt I had remained calm, confident, and strong throughout the day of driving, waiting, and testing, but the sight of the abandoned birthday cake, children's cards, and piles of sloppily wrapped gifts on a dining room table, all waiting to be celebrated with their father, collapsed me to tears.

In less than twelve hours my plans for a birthday celebration changed into plans for recovery and prayers for a longer life. Lighting a single candle on the chocolate cake, I sat down alone and prayed for thirty-nine more years of life and love.

When I crawled into bed later, I grabbed my small book of prayers. The reading for the day was a letter written to a friend by St. Francis de Sales (1567-1622):

"Do not look forward to the changes or chances of this life in fear.
Rather, look to them with full hope, that, as they arise,
God, whose you are, will deliver you out of them.
He has kept you hitherto – hold fast to his dear hand,
and He will lead you safely through all things;
And, when you cannot stand, He will bear you in His arms.

Do not look forward to what may happen tomorrow;
The same everlasting Father who cares for you today,

will take care of you tomorrow, and every day.
Either He will shield you from suffering,
or He will give you unfailing strength to bear it.
Be at peace then,
and put aside all anxious thoughts and imaginations."

I returned to that passage each morning and evening for nearly a year following the stroke. I practiced the advice by writing notes of gratitude. Neighbor's shoveled snow... a friend brought milk... a co-worker cleaned my bathroom...relatives cared for our children... Several nurses commented that I appeared to have great serenity during the stressful weeks of testing and difficult decisions. They wondered how I remained so calm. The way I saw it was that the grace of gratitude was beginning to show.

Jack's aortic valve was later replaced. To this day, he continues running as a cardiac athlete. But the lessons from the "stroke-birthday" remain a touchstone for my life and faith. I write thoughts of gratitude at the end of each day, and especially when a current situation seems difficult, or I begin to feel anxious about the changes or chances in life, I bring to mind that January day. I re-read the prayer of St. Francis de Sales. Then, I open my gratitude journal and begin to write.

Linda Berkery is a spiritual director and pastoral associate. She contributed reflections to: *Learning Life through Funerals, The Life-Givers, Amnesia* and *Reconciliation,* and fiction: *Broken Glass-Mended He*arts, for *Liguorian,* a national Catholic magazine, and various newspapers. Linda grew up in a funeral home and married her high school sweetheart.

A PROMISE TO KEEP

Doris Thome

Her voice is weak and hesitant. "I . . . didn't faint. Did I?" I shake my head. "No," my voice thick with emotion. A period of silence settles over us like a protective cloak until Kelsey's curiosity gets the better of her.

"Is that what it will be like?"

"Was that scary for you?" I respond.

"No. It was so fast. I actually left. I…"

"That is what death is like. Dying can be slow and peaceful or long and difficult. Some drift into unconsciousness. Or it can be fast, as you experienced."

This was familiar territory to me, as I had been a nurse for over forty years.

It had been a few weeks since my hospice rounds included Kelsey, whose ashy blond hair and gorgeous green eyes resemble so closely those of her handsome father. I can only imagine that she is sorely missed by all the teeny boppers at her high school.

Just four months ago fifteen-year-old Kelsey was diagnosed with stage V cancer, a terminal state. Too late to excise the mass, a colostomy had to be performed. Her family had frantically opted for chemotherapy. The harsh drugs were too toxic for young Kelsey. She begged them to stop. On target with what a terminal patient experiences, I have seen Kelsey deal with denial, anger, bargaining and acceptance in surprisingly rapid succession and true to form she now vacillates, one moment displaying anger, the next accepting reality and, in no time back to denial.

Kelsey's father and stepmother, Liz, review with me Kelsey's latest changes. Armed with the girl's condition and the parent's insight, I tap on her bedroom door. Hearing a response, I enter. Despite her parent's optimistic report, I'm surprised that Kelsey has lost considerable weight and appears groggy. I can't help thinking of my own children when they were her age. Despite all the research and money spent there is still nothing our medical community can do if cancer of the bowel becomes invasive and is not detected early.

Under the bedcovers, where her colostomy appliance rests, I notice a mound. I know this means excessive gas has built up in her colostomy bag. As I approach the hospital bed to check, I say, "How are you, sleepy head?"

Kelsey barely manages to say, "Hi Jessie," before a giant yawn overtakes her.

"Excuse me. Were you out on the town last night?"

"I wish. A few of my friends came by. Dad ordered pizza and Liz brought in sodas and made popcorn. It was fun and turned into a late night, I guess." Kelsey doesn't realize her friends had left well before 9:00 p.m.

"And this, young lady, is what soda does. This colostomy bag is ready to blast off."

Kelsey listens wide-eyed.

An exploding bag, or one that comes loose from its site, is an event every colostomy owner experiences at least once. It is something they never want to repeat. As I empty Kelsey's colostomy bag, first of its gas then of the stool, I feel her cooled extremities, observe her mottled skin and notice her nail beds are blue-tinged – all signs of reduced circulation. I clean up her colostomy supplies, scrub my hands and cautiously massage the deep creases her linens formed across her back and hips.

"All this feels great but I can't lie here anymore." Kelsey moans. "I need to get out of this bed and sit up for a while. Can I get up now?"

I move to the other side of the bed to assist and observe her. As she pushes the button to raise the head of the bed, I notice there are no linens for me to use and signal for her to wait. As I open the bedroom door to request fresh linens, Kelsey moves her legs to dangle them over the edge of the mattress.

"Here are some sheets," says Liz, as Kelsey's parents enter the room.

As I turn to reach for the linens, the facial expressions of both parents suddenly become torturous masks. I spin around, then lunge toward Kelsey. Drained of color, she is in free fall. Blocking her descent, I simultaneously catch her and yell for her dad to lower the head of the bed. Lowering her trunk, I lift the girl's legs onto the bed. She's not breathing. I rush to raise the foot of the bed into the Trendelenburg position, where the body is laid supine with the feet higher than the head.

Color rushes back into Kelsey's face. She gasps for air then opens her eyes. Surprised and watchful, she blinks and attempts to process what has just occurred.

"What just happened?"

"Oh honey, you fainted, that's all," Liz says, her emotion in check.

I make my demeanor radiate calmness but adrenalin still races through my body over what happened when I asked Kelsey's parents for a change of linens. A mere seven steps away from her bed and how long – fifteen seconds? And look what happened.

Once Kelsey is stabilized, with me on one side and her father on the other, we assist her to transfer to the overstuffed armchair.

"Call us if you need anything," says Kelsey's father as he joins Liz, then shuts the door behind him.

For safety, I move the bedside table in front of my patient and press down the wheel locks. As I strip and remake her hospital bed I observe her closely. Deep in thought Kelsey sits, oblivious to her surroundings. I think she's replaying what just happened.

I move a straight-back chair to position myself across from Kelsey's tray table. My closeness attracts her attention and brings her back from wherever her mind had strayed.

But Kelsey immediately breaks eye contact with a seriousness so intense that the hum of her thoughts seem to vibrate into the room. Is she frightened? I wonder. Unsure? Both? Kelsey does not lift her head, instead she peeks, quick glances, up through her lashes. Then soul-wrenching green irises and coal-black pupils lock onto mine. I wish I could take her fear away. Yet I know it's time to speak the words so difficult to hear. I steady myself; I will my pulse to slow, to become calm.

"Are you aware of what happened to you earlier?" I ask, my tone quiet and unemotional

Kelsey nods that she understands then asks, "Is it common for patients like me to dream about people who have died?"

"For terminal patients?"

"Yeah, terminal," she says quietly

"It is very common," I reply.

"I see my Mom all the time and we have great conversations. She can't wait to show me around, says there's a whole bunch of people watching over me... even some kids my age. But some of the others... Geez, I dream of grandparents, great grandparents, even people I haven't met."

"What are they like?"

"I really like my Grandpa Jake. He's cool and he knows so much... interesting stuff that I like... astronomy, oceanography. He was a geologist."

I grin, struck by Kelsey's perception.

"What?" she asks me, wanting to know what I'm thinking.

"I love what happens to young people, even very young children."

"About what?"

"Terminal children acquire an awareness," I say, "a kind of instinctive wisdom, the same that I see in the very old who have so few generational companions left and so tend to identify more with those friends and loved ones who have died. They wake and wonder where their husband or best friend has gone."

By now, Kelsey's color is the best I've seen since I arrived. She's invigorated and opening up beautifully. Who would have guessed that the frightening experience we had earlier would have produced such acceptance.

"Jessie, do people really get wiser as they get older?"

"Yes and no. Wisdom comes from experiences and how one views these events. Remember your first broken heart?""Trevor… Oh boy, do I"

"What did you learn from how Trevor treated you?"

"I don't know but it felt awful. Ashamed. Embarrassed. It changed me, made me leery, and I remember when some boy asked me to a dance, I told him, 'No way…' not a polite, 'No thank you,' but a nasty, 'Get lost, no way.' Before I knew Trevor, when we were hangin' at the mall, these two guys asked me and my friend Alisha out."

Kelsey puts her hands over her face. "We were horrible… laughed at them, called them names. I guess we thought we were so great. But Trevor showed me how much things like that hurt."

"And now?"

"I get it. Now I accept or refuse . . . I guess you'd say… and with a lot more tact too."

"Ah, you learned. You make better choices. So my answer to your question is that some elders, like some teenagers, learn from life. And yes, they become wise."

There's that look again. Kelsey's mind is working on another concern. "That episode, Jessie… What happened to me earlier? That was a kind of dress rehearsal, wasn't it?"

"Gee, I guess it was. Does that bother you?"

"No way. Not now, but my folks were really freaked out, big time. Would you talk to them? I don't know how to explain it. Let them know everything'll be okay."

"Will it?"

"Yeah, I think it will. I thought dying would be painful, like suffocating. But yeah, it will be okay. You will talk to them? Promise me?"

Kelsey is ready, but her folks are not and this lovely girl will slip away soon. I'm finished here but I've a promise to keep – a promise to Kelsey.

Doris Thome: See Bio following *Final Adventure*.

LIFE

Jeannette Caruth

The whirling of the clock is slowing down …
our bowl of expectations is being emptied
and the gentle truth is being revealed.
We discover what it is we do not care for,
we have come to know what does not work for us
and so the process of elimination has come to a quiet fruition
in the springtime of the last phase of our life.
Simplicity has absorbed chaos,
contentment has made the intensity of desire obsolete,
openness has melted the pursuit of righteousness,
today has swallowed tomorrow.
The peace of not-wanting deepens,
the joy of not-needing enlightens.
The beauty of age has silenced the tools
for sculpturing our lives
and in this breathless silence
the song of an unimaginable freedom is being heard.
And while the outer beauty folds its magic wings,
the inner beauty has taken its virgin flight
into unchartered territories.

The cycle is complete …
The madness understood …
And with the understanding
all has been transformed into Love.
Life fulfills its own purpose
and celebrates itself.

In her native Holland, Jeannette Caruth first fell in love with poetry and dance: ballet. The fluidity of this love brought her effortlessly to the dance of visual images and she became a painter. Simultaneously, words started to flow into poetry, embraced by these various expressions, she found the Art of Living.

PART 5

My Body; My Mind; My Spirit; Myself

"The great secret that all old people share is that you really haven't changed in 70 or 80 years. Your body changes, but you don't change at all."

Doris Lessing

A KIND OF MAGIC

R J. Burnhart

"Slow down, Phil, I'm trying to catch up to you." I accelerate my pace but my breathing is hard. I'm drenched with sweat. I can even feel what is left of my fast-thinning hair plastered flat against my forehead and the back of my neck. "Phil, you remember me, don't you? Arch. Arch McCleary." I shift my gym bag to the other shoulder. "Hey man, you're looking at me as if you've never seen me before. Good grief, have I changed that much?"

I can tell Phil is struggling to remember who I am. I am only a few months past sixty six, but if it's that hard to recognize me, I must be in a lot worse shape than I thought. When I knew Phil – about six or seven years ago – I had energy to burn and a great athletic body.

"Phil, I've been looking for you. The company Doc is telling me I need to take a good aerobics or yoga class – one geared to my age. I'm so out of shape, my neck feels fused to my body like its rusted rock solid." Then I cut myself short not wanting to say too much. I don't want him to know that I'm beginning to feel like I'm a danger to myself and maybe everybody else. If the cops knew how run down my body has become, sitting for hours at my computer, they'd yank my driver's license in a nanosecond. I can't even turn my head around when I'm driving to see what's behind me.

"Tell you what, Arch, come along to class at your own pace. When you get to the gym, find yourself a space on the floor. Then take a minute to relax. Do some good, deep breathing while you wait for the class to begin.

I'll be relieved if Phil never learns the worst of it, like the way I can hardly draw a deep breath, or stand for any length of time without looking around for something to lean against. So what if the company doc tells me the ole ticker's doing OK. My problem is I feel lousy. Odd aches. Shooting pains. Swelling legs. I'm frankly tired of looking at every boring day through clouded glasses. I have to push myself to get up in the morning let alone find anything that's even worth so much as a fraction of a smile. This class better be good. It's costing me, what with having to leave work thirty minutes early and fighting the traffic to make it here on time. Good grief, I'm sweaty. And, what's with this getting down on the mat? Question is, will I be able to get up again?

Phil is telling us, "DMV will say it's not smart to rely only on your rearview mirror when driving. There's nothing better than our own eyes, so let's start with some easy twists. Let's let the ole body know whose boss. Everybody, please stand and come to the front of your mat, and if you see someone who could use a hand, reach out."

I'm glad I met Della. She's spread out her mat beside me. She looks like a human block and tackle and that's what I need close by.

"Now stand straight, feet shoulder-width apart, shoulders up, back, and down. Get your balance. First, stand with palms facing your sides. Feel your body. Become acquainted with it. Begin to let it speak to you. Now, without moving anything else, merely turn your palms outward. My question to all of you is: how has this simple gesture influenced your body?" The room is silent. "Makes you stand up still straighter, right? You feel it in your shoulders and down the spine, correct? This is an example of how even the slightest, focused movement can work for a positive effect on the body. Keep this in mind, now let's move on . . ."

That was simple, but I can't believe what I have done to myself. This is scary. I used to run the kids' marathons, played basketball with them at the Y. I'm only in my sixties and I'm not a drinker. I don't smoke. I don't take drugs. How could my body change on me so fast – and so radically?"

"If you need some support, take one of those metal folding chairs over by the side of the room. Don't be shy. We start where you're at and from there we move forward."

I'm dizzy. I notice my energy is draining out of me with each stretching and tensing pose I do. I'll be glad when we get to the end of this class. Even with the support of the chair, I feel ridiculously out of my league. My arm joints are stuck. They refuse to let me stretch them straight up above my head. And bending at the waist? Forget that. Stomach's like a wad of styrofoam. How do some of these women here do all this? They're no younger than I am. In fact, mostly older, is my guess.

"Make a commitment and hang in. See you next time," Phil tells us and just like that the class is finally over. "And Arch, could you stop by a minute before you leave?"

I don't want to talk to Phil about this. What can I say to him? Life isn't working for me. I know that, and I don't want to be cornered into having to talk about it. Ever since Carla left and the firm began their waves of cutbacks, I've had nothing but anger and frustration. I'm left with the work of six guys, plus running the house, and also paying the kids' college tuition. How could Carla do this to me? I've had to fight the urge to call the children right out of their college classes and tell them about the witch their mother's turned into for up and taking off. She says she wants some time to find herself. To me, that's being a bitch. Could've kicked a hole in the bedroom wall. Even now, I still have to hold myself back from gathering up the jewelry I've given her over the years and tossing it on E-bay. But oh no, not me. I'll be at the office every morning at eight a.m. sharp – no, probably twenty minutes earlier, because it takes me so long just to rip the cobwebs out of my head and focus on my work for the day. I'll pay the tuitions, and the mortgage, and the utilities – on time like always.

"Sure, sure, Phil, I'll be at the next class, but sorry, I gotta go now. I'll catch up with you next time." I keep my head down and head for the door.

So week after week, I drag my sorry body to class, spread out my mat, and force myself to do the moves Phil directs. Is it hell? Can't imagine anything worse. I never talk with Phil after class. I make a point to concoct excuse after excuse to get out of that gym - fast.

Two months later I reluctantly go for my medical check-up. "Blood pressure is in the normal range, Arch. You've dropped thirteen pounds," Doc Stern tells me. "And as for your posture, do you ever notice how you look straight into the eyes of the person you're talking to now instead of looking up at them from a hunched over position? Things are looking good, friend. We'll follow this up with a blood test. Want to check the cholesterol levels and make sure the chemistry is balanced."

Sure I notice my belt is going a little slack, but so what? Just adjust the buckle's all I have to do. As I am about to leave, Doc Stern says, "And by the way, Arch, keep it up. You're about to prove to yourself the incredible resilience of the human body no matter what the age, or what the starting condition. It looks like we're talking mind over body here. I'm impressed, my friend."

Frankly, I have never given much attention to the power my thoughts have over anything except the mathematical formulas I work with in my profession. I'm an Engineer. I know my stuff. I live up to my commitments (more than I can say about some people in my life). What matters to me has always been how I meet problems and how I come up with ways to solve them, and collect my salary check in the process. I try to keep life as black and white as possible. The grey stuff is for somebody else, not me

And, yet, there's no denying what the test results are showing. I've even begun to notice how calming deep breathing can be, and the way my body is beginning to feel after a good workout of stretching and flexing and accelerating the ole cardio. As for ratcheting up the heart rate, man I can pump out the sweat – even if it does make me reek like a hippo.

On occasion I even feel an up-beat, euphoric sensation, like the time Phil had us stand on our mats, our feet a shoulder-width apart. Then he directed us to interlace our fingers and bring our arms high above our heads.

"Higher. Higher. Higher," he encouraged us and I noticed how my elbow joints are more flexible now. "OK, lean back and force your chest up. Further. Further. Up. Up. Reach up higher. Now, see yourself setting your heart free. With that, I felt a sudden sensation like the whole front of me was opening up. Like my heart was expanding – way beyond my chest – radiating an incredible feeling. How can I say it any other way . . . it felt like joy. Simple, kid-like joy. Even my imagination let go – felt like some angel was dipping its wing my way and I was finally doing something right.

But I still have to deal with my head. I don't like what's been going on in there. Too dreary. Too dark. I know now it doesn't have to be this way. I can't believe this is what a few simple exercises can do.

⌒

"It's going to be our own version of Happy Hour," Della says to me at the next class. "Come along. Join us. Only an hour or so. We're going to sip veggie juice and hold our stomachs – as in laughing, of course. We'll work in a little counting of our blessings, and seeing the zany side of our lives, but basically, we'll just have good relaxed fun. No pressure."

The only part of what she says that gives me a shout-out is her last point. I need no more pressure. As for the rest of it, well who knows, maybe a little New Age woo-woo stuff can be put up with. I can give it a try.

⌒

"Before we get started on today's exercises, let me ask you a few questions," says Phil at the next class. "Don't speak out your answer; just think about what I'm asking. Tell me this: How is your energy these days? Your balance? Keeping up with a good diet? How about your water in-take? Sleep regimen working for you? Are you consciously taking a moment here, another there, just long enough to sit quietly? Maybe smell some flowers? Got good friends? How much laughing have you done today? How much just savoring the moment?"

Right there. That's where Phil gets to me. Along with all these other seniors sitting here on the gym floor, I believe every one of us at this very moment, is savoring exactly where we are and how we are: Centered. Grounded. Alone, yet with others we've come to like, to really care about. Right here in a space where all is as it is, and as it should be because we've plainly said to ourselves we're going to commit to our health and ourselves. It's up to each of us. And that's that.

The late afternoon sun spreads out from the windows across the gym floor. Faces glow in its light. We've been together as a class a little more than seven months and an amazing amount has happened in that brief time. I've become energized; I've come to know tranquility – and the awesome sense of OK-ness – a kind that settles in around me. As for savoring the moment and letting the feeling sit with me, I wonder why Phil has never spoken before about this dimension of things – like an exponential expansion of the spirit – a kind of magic.

I'll have to stop after class and mention this to him.

Engineer and advocate for senior fitness.

*"We don't stop playing because we grow old.
We grow old because we stop playing."*

George Bernard Shaw

GETTING BACK IN THE SADDLE

Leslie A. Westbrook

"Women need a reason to have sex, men just need a place." — Billy Crystal

After three and a half years of casual online dating, I finally came across a fella on Match.com who sparked my interest, largely because *he* was interested in things beyond candlelit dinners and sunset walks on the beach. After I read his amusing and engaging profile (and the photo wasn't bad), my intuition said, "This could be the one."

I sent him a simple greeting and asked what movies and types of music he liked (those, and political leanings, are my litmus test). A flurry of emails led to a lively — and encouraging — phone conversation, which led to plans to meet for lunch. Over bowls of clam chowder in a restaurant overlooking a boat harbor, our first date lasted three hours.

My insecurities kicked in about halfway through the meal. *This guy is attractive, and funny and upbeat and, wow, I think I could really like him,* I thought to myself, while a deeper interior voice screamed, "*Oh my god, he can't possibly like* me, *and if he does, how do I tell him it's been eons since I've been intimate with anyone?"* Obviously, this was not a conversation I was ready to have, but I'd be lying if I didn't admit it was very much on my mind.

Let's-call-him-Sam wanted to meet again. And again. After spending quite a bit of time together and exchanging a few kisses and doing some cuddling on a cold winter's night, I blurted out a confession.

"Sam, I really like you, but I am scared to death about making love with you. I am not sure it will work physically for me. A few years ago my gynecologist told me to 'use it or lose it' or I would only be able to accommodate something the size of a pencil. More importantly," I continued in what felt like one long run-on sentence, "I am frightened that physical intimacy might ruin our great friendship."

What I didn't admit was that I wasn't sure I was "all in" just yet.

And, if I'm being totally honest, despite having really enjoyed making love over the centuries (20th and 21st) I wondered whether I was even that interested. My hormone levels had clearly dropped off, and I hadn't been feeling as sexually ... *charged* ... as I was in my younger days. Was Mother Nature shutting down ye olde baby making factory in some sort of cosmic joke, I wondered?

I wondered if my physical and emotional fears of intimacy might chase him away. But the more we talked and spent time together, the more secure I felt that he was willing to wait to see if my ability to commit - physically and emotionally - might evolve. As Billy Crystal noted, I needed all the reasons in my head to be aligned, much like the stars that had brought us together in the first place.

Sam had dated a bit over the past few years - after having divorced from a 20-year marriage. He had run scared from the women who had pursued him, including one (the mother of children his grown children's ages) who came around with homemade lasagna, another who wore too much make-up and yet another who was OCD. He kept telling me that he was "wild" about me - and he was interested in a full-blown relationship (no pun intended). "I do better with a partner," he said, making me feel oh-so-special.

"What are *your* fears?" I asked the 60-year-old. I was careful not to bring up the physical challenges some older men experience, like erectile dysfunction or leaky or premature ejaculation. Being a typical male, Sam responded: "I don't want to look at someone who is my age because I don't want to be reminded how old I am. It's not the age- it's the mileage. I don't care if somebody is 45 or 65. If they look old – and have lines and wrinkles or look horrible without make up, it's a turn off. Everybody looks the same in the dark, but they don't feel the same." Oy vey. Well, neither one of us were spring chickens. And I certainly am not Dorian Gray, although people often comment I look young for my age. Fear of physical aging sounded like his fear to me.

"What's important to you?" I continued with my inquiries.

"Comfort level and chemistry, whether a woman is a brain surgeon or a waitress. Physical and intellectual attraction and emotional comfort," he said, admitting that he was aware that his current living "circumstances" were uncomfortable for both of us.

I worried that too much candor about such a delicate subject could put a damper on things. But I also hoped it might have the opposite effect and stimulate the kind of dialogue that would create a deeper intimacy than either one of us had ever experienced.

Part of my consternation stemmed from the fact that since I was no longer a raging hormonal machine, my rational mind had a bigger say in my choice of a partner than in my past. My needs for a sexual partner and mate had "evolved." Now that I've reached the age where I can start withdrawing from my Roth IRA (59½), and ever since the cost of my health insurance jumped 26 percent, I found that what turns me on is a man who is not only honest, intelligent, fun, thoughtful and sexually attractive but one who has a steady income, health care coverage and a good retirement plan. Being truthful, my security needs seem to play a large role in terms of how much I was willing to "play ball."

While Sam had all the wonderful human attributes I craved – plus he was super handy around the house and loved to "fix" things, as well as cook and was great at clean-up – his health insurance was about to run out, his 17-year-old BMW he had inherited from his mother sounded like a herd of elephants when it started, and it was leaking oil and transmission fluids all over my driveway. He had been job-hunting for regular employment with benefits after his previous employer had gone bankrupt. When we met originally (in the boat harbor) he had painted a romantic picture of his abilities as a boat captain and sailing instructor for the past 20 years, but that business had failed. He was renting a room at a "sailing buddy's" house where he was too embarrassed to invite me over and I had not met any of his friends, family or co-workers, which was a real red flag in the "I want to get intimate with you department."

Sure, sex can be spontaneous, but without trust, love, a sense of safety and some careful planning, at least for this romantic, it's just another toss in the hay, which may appeal to some, but not to this fledgling romantic.

The ice was beginning to melt for me and I was beginning to feel more amorous. But just after "Sam" had prepared a romantic and delicious Valentine's Day dinner of lobster tails, risotto with porcini mushrooms, a tasty and healthy kale salad, and broccoli from my garden paired with lovely wines, his knee went out. In pain and having difficulty getting up and down and moving about, I feared there would be no hanky-panky from his side of the equation/bed in our near future. Which brought up an entirely other issue regarding the "physical challenges" of sex after 60. Our moving parts don't always function the same way as they did in our youth - be it our genitalia, our hips, our knees as well as our brains.

The following day I was scheduled for my annual physical and, when I told my doctor about the physical part of my dilemma, he immediately offered to write me a prescription for Estrace or Premarin cream.

"I think I will wait," I said to him.

"Just call me when you are ready," he replied. I wanted to do some research, as I knew that Premarin was NOT good news for women.

While I was considering going further, Sam, despite his bad knee remained hopeful.

He emailed me: "There are numerous positions that don't involve my knee. And I can't think of anything I'd rather do than test a few of them out. I'm sure we can get very creative and never risk injury to my knee or other body parts. READY WHEN YOU ARE BABY!"

The problem was, I was never really ready to go all the way with Sam. We did remain friends and there's a lot to be said for friendship. Maybe it was evident early on and I was trying to push something that I didn't really feel. I thought all I had to do was align my brain with his knee, be ready to get the right creams and then let Sam know. But love and intimacy aren't that simple, at least not for me.

Sam got hired for a job out of hundreds of applicants, but he quit the job after a few weeks. About a year later, he found his dream job as the captain of a large, historic yacht that he is restoring from stem to stern and then he will be sailing from California to the Mediterranean.

I get seasick and obviously things weren't meant to be between us. But meeting Sam made me realize that I could almost fall for someone again. And maybe next time, all the stars will align for intimacy, as well as friendship and companionship, and I will hop back in the saddle and move slowly and tenderly (with a little help in the hormone department) towards that thing called love.

Leslie A. Westbrook is a third generation Californian who has been a newspaper columnist, magazine editor and freelance writer for most of her adult life. She has written books and articles on travel, the 100-year history of a college, design and weird people she has known. A different version of this essay appeared on NextAvenue.org. She resides in Central California. Her website is www.LeslieWestbrook.com

A WELL NIGH UNATTAINABLE IDEAL

A Retrospective

Susan Chan Egan

Difficult to imagine, but foreign students were something of a rarity on American campuses forty years ago. For non-Asian males, I was a specimen of that mythical creature, the Oriental girl at once imperious, compliant, mystifying, and sexy. I had been ashamed of my dark skin in the Philippines, where I grew up, and Taiwan, where I attended two years of college. In Asia, pale was prized and I found it incredulous that my sorority sisters exposed themselves to the sun for hours just to get tanned. Consciously or subconsciously, I began to play up to the expectation of being somewhat exotic. Barely five feet two and thin as a rail, I let my hair grow long, took to wearing short, short skirts and sporting a wide arm bracelet. I dated a very tall blond guy with a red beard from Finland, who, I believe was, like so many, motivated by curiosity and novelty.

I chose the University of Washington in large part because, at a dinner party in Taipei, I met the remarkable woman,

Isabella Yen, running the Chinese language program there. She was a diminutive woman with a warm handshake and a voice that resembled chiming bells, who exuded vitality despite being a hunchback due to a childhood accident. The university had arranged a host family for every foreign student. Mine were the Burgetts. I didn't live with them but they were helpful in providing me with social insights and instruction.

For the first two months in Seattle, I lodged at a rooming house near campus trying to make my meager savings stretch as far as possible. My money worries vanished overnight when Chi Omega Sorority offered me free room and board. I could hardly believe my good fortune.

It was 1969 and all sorts of barriers were crumbling. American youths, called upon to fight an unpopular war, rose up to challenge their parents' long-held assumptions and, in their disillusionment, searched for alternative realities. This was the era of civil disobedience, manifestos and flower children. "Make love, not war!" was the rallying cry – the "love" part having been made an easy proposition by the new availability of contraceptives. I did not yet know I was about to join the ranks of America's baby boomers, marked by our defiance of authority, our self-indulgence, as well as our idealism. I felt like a little duckling born in the woods that, waddling along, somehow found its way to the pond.

I was dazzled by America's wealth and shocked by its profligacy, the copious use of paper towels and throwaway dinnerware, the astounding selection of pet food in supermarkets. I learned to operate washing machines and make my bed with a top sheet and fitted bottom sheet. I learned not to tell people they had put on weight—a compliment in Chinese. I learned to run barefoot in the grass. I was introduced to the Beatles. I took to humming "Raindrops keep fallin' on my head" in cold Seattle drizzles. However the closest I got to drugs was sniffing heavy whiffs of marijuana drifting my way at a rock concert.

I made new friends—males and females, European, African, Asians, as well as Americans. My closest male friend was an Irish-American with a touch of old-world chivalry named Ronald Christopher Egan. A native of Connecticut, driven to the west coast by his parents' bitter divorce, Ron had majored in English at the University of California in Santa Barbara, where he supported himself teaching sailing. To fulfill the university's foreign language requirement, he took, as a joke, Chinese, because he did badly in French during high school. His Chinese teacher, however, saw promise in him and encouraged him to switch his major to Chinese. By the end of his junior year, he had exhausted the limited number of Chinese courses then being offered, and his teacher took him to Taiwan for intensive study, after which he went up the coast to the University of Washington to study with Helmut Wilhelm, a highly respected scholar born in China. It was in Professor Wilhelm's class that we met. Ron later told me I always arrived late to class and then showed off by correcting the Chinese characters Professor Wilhelm scribbled on the blackboard. I had no idea how ornery I was because Professor Wilhelm, a mild-mannered German gentleman, and always dressed in a three-piece suit, never let on he was annoyed.

My conversations with Ron would often start after class and lasted into late afternoons, whereupon he would ask me out to dinner. He professed to admire me for my honesty. To reciprocate, I had him over to Chi Omega for formal Wednesday night dinners, at which we were supposed to introduce our male friends to the housemother, presumably for her approval. Just like my college dormitory in Taiwan, Chi Omega required male guests to announce themselves, so that the girls, summoned over the intercom, could meet them at the reception room. However, unlike our dormitory in Taiwan, Chi Omega had a spacious living room graced with a grand piano, where we could entertain our male guests, and where the rule of "no hand-holding within three blocks of the House" was flouted with glee. But Ron was three years younger than I. I did not consider him my beau, simply a friend with whom I enjoyed endless conversations.

"How could he afford to take you out to dinner all the time?" I was taken aback when one of my roommates asked me. I said I didn't know. It never occurred to me to inquire. I learned later that Ron, when he ate by himself, limited himself to Mrs. Paul's Fish Sticks. The big question was whether to splurge and have four fish sticks, or to eat three so that he could stretch the package of twelve over four meals. He took me once to where he lodged in the attic of a picturesque house. I was impressed by how neatly and tastefully he arranged his room.

There was, at the University District's last exit to the freeway, a coffeehouse named fittingly The Last Exit. It featured a band and poetry readings. One evening, while Ron and I were there, the audience was invited to the platform to recite poems. At Ron's urging, I went up and recited a poem in Chinese. As I sat down to his twinkling eyes and approving smile, I pondered the startling possibility of being hitched to a man unafraid of being upstaged by a woman.

Ron had not taken any class with Isabella Yen but she had noticed him. When he was kicked out by his landlord, a frugal old man ever leery of being bilked, for baking a single potato in the oven, Isabella Yen, under the mistaken impression that Ron and I were going steady, took him in to live with her and her physicist husband Kao Shu-koo. He and Dr. Kao shared a reverence for woodwork, taking special delight in jerry-rigged solutions to tricky carpentry problems. Ron's and my path happened to converge at a time when we could best appreciate each other.

On returning from Christmas vacation, Ron told me he showed my picture to his parents in Connecticut. He asked if I might spend the coming summer with him in Santa Barbara where he was to run a sailing program for teenagers. When I mentioned his invitation to Isabella she urged me, to my great surprise, to accept. Still, I hesitated. This is not how I was brought up. What does all this mean? Ron did not exactly propose. Does this imply I'm committed to him for life? Would I be marked as a fallen woman? Disgraced? My parents certainly would not have approved.

Soon afterwards, as Isabella and I walked down the sidewalk, we saw a woman with an adorable Eurasian child. Isabella smiled and said, "With any luck, you will have a child looking like her."

Following what became an idyllic summer in Santa Barbara with Ron, I returned to Seattle and to Chi Omega in the fall to pursue a master's degree in comparative literature. I focused on literary criticism because I wanted to understand why words have the power to sway us even in our sleep.

Much later, our daughter, then a teenager, once asked me how Daddy proposed and was initially appalled, then proud, to learn I was the one who popped the question. How it happened was Ron and I were sitting upright in our sleeping bags in front of the fireplace at the Burgetts' living room late one night. Sensing how Ron felt about me, I said out of the blue, as I watched the flames leaping and sputtering, that having been in

America for such a short time I was not ready to make any long-term commitment. I saw his face fall as he said quietly, "You may wake up one day and find me gone." Suddenly the idea that we might drift apart, like tiny boats in an ocean of humanity, and never cross paths again, became inconceivable. I found myself saying, a tad sharply, "We might as well get married!"

Ron's mother Ruth was gracious enough not to let on how shocked she was about this—aside from the fact that Ron was not quite twenty-two, and I am Asian. No one in her social circle had done anything nearly so outlandish. Later, she wrote saying she had a ring for me and she asked me for a picture to announce our engagement in the *Westport News*.

My parents would have much preferred a Chinese son-in-law; I know that. But I was no longer dependent on their support, and being thousands of miles away, there was really nothing they could do. They would have been exceedingly upset if I were to marry a Filipino, but an American was so far out of the norm they did not know what to make of it. The only objection they raised was that Ron was younger than I. They were also concerned with the high rate of American divorce, which was unheard of among people we knew. They were, no doubt, relieved to see me settle down, to hear the man to whom I had imprudently attached myself was willing to marry me. At my suggestion, Ron wrote my grandmother a letter in Chinese asking for her blessing, which pleased her.

At the Marriage Licensing Office, the King County Clerk had asked routinely if we were related to each other, prompting Ron to ask, "Do we look like we are related?"

Not only do we look different, we differ in our physical response to our surroundings. Being exceptionally alive to sights, sounds, smells and textures, along with an unerring sense of balance, are what make Ron a champion sailor. On the other hand, I could hardly pour anything without spilling and live much of my life enveloped in a fog of abstraction. I drink tea; he drinks coffee. I prefer the house warm, he likes it cold. Our disparate upbringing is most evident at buffet dinners where we invariably choose different food. The mound of meat, beans, and potatoes ending up on his plate and the heap of shellfish on mine hint at the kind of compromises we make on a daily basis.

Life has taken us across three continents. We raised a child, struggled with our parents, and underwent various personal metamorphoses, evolving into individuals hardly recognizable to our younger selves. Through the turmoil of more than four decades our conversations never cease. Our shared delight in words has helped us stay together.

Ron and I did not know we were at the forefront of a huge trend. A recent study by the Pew Research Center found nearly one in six new marriages in the United States are now interracial. Our Chinese-Irish daughter is happily married to a man whose parents emigrated from Romania. Even black-white couples are so commonplace that, in most parts of the country, they no longer raise eyebrows or turn heads. Before too long, America will truly be a melting pot, stereotypes dissolved and skin colors blended away. Perhaps salad is a better metaphor, all mixed up with each ingredient contributing distinct flavor to its richness. Nowhere else in the world is this mixing and blending happening at this rate. That's why I am optimistic about America.

I now consider myself an American, more precisely a Chinese-American who grew up in Manila. What is the most difficult adjustment I have had to make over the past four decades? Looking back, I believe it involves personal boundaries.

Most Americans generally see themselves as individuals. The relationships between individuals are usually well defined. People mind their own business and expect others to mind theirs. One does not normally take in sick friends or impoverished relatives, even if there might be plenty of room in the house.

Asians, on the other hand, are brought up as members of a clan. Close friends become honorary members of the clan, being called "Big Sister Such and Such" or "Uncle Such and Such" even though no blood relation exists. Within the clan, life is basically communal, with the better off expected to take care of the less fortunate. Generosity is remembered and grudges held, sometimes for generations. The givers earn gratitude and respect and, more often than not, the right to call in their chips. This web of mutual obligations tends to serve society well in the absence of a social welfare system.

Thus, one often sees what appears to be a scuffle breaking out at Chinese restaurants, with diners trying to grab the bill at the end of a meal. The subtext of the wrangle may include: "Let *me* pay because I have more money." "Don't *you* underestimate me! I am richer than you think." "C'mon, we are old friends and I view you as family." "Heck, we just happened to run into each other. Darn if I let myself become obligated to you." Eventually, a face-saving device is usually found, such as one party claiming it is his treat because he wants to celebrate the birth of a grandson.

What is viewed as kindness in one culture may be considered presumptuous in the other. I had to learn when to keep my distance out of respect for others' privacy, to learn what was and was not socially acceptable to say and do.

When she was a two-year-old, my daughter would often wrap her arms around me and say, "Mommy, when I grow up, I will be you!"

My heart always skipped a beat when she said that. Would I want her to be like me? I was shaped by a culture where there was very little margin for error. Break a leg and you are crippled for life. All activities had to be directed toward survival. We are all shaped, perhaps more accurately, warped by our background. Would this be the case with my daughter?

To a large extent, I slipped through myriad cultural barriers by being blissfully unaware of them, having bought naively and wholeheartedly into the American ideal of equality for all.

Although I now realize the American ideal of equality is just that, an ideal, well-nigh unattainable, still I firmly believe it is worth striving for. By acknowledging we all have the same needs and aspirations, still we see through the superficiality of ethnic characteristics and cultural mores. Recognizing our common humanity often allows us to transcend our backgrounds. A habit of seeing others as equals and—more importantly—seeing herself as equal to everyone else is my wish for my Irish-Chinese American daughter. Indeed, it is my wish for all sentient beings young and old. Why not treat all people as equals even though, in an imperfect world, they are not? It is a good habit that brings out the best in all of us.

A retired securities analyst, Susan Chan Egan, is author of *A Latterday Confucian* and its Chinese editions, co-author of *A Pragmatist and His Free Spirit*, and co-translator of *The Song of Everlasting Sorrow*. She is working on a memoir of the American experience of her Chinese family from Manila.

LET THE SMALL CLOCKS RUN WILD

A MEDITATION

Ronald Pies M.D.

The great clock of your life
is slowing down,
and the small clocks run wild.
For this you were born.
  –Stanley Kunitz, *King of the River*

So now the woods have opened up a bit, even as they have darkened, and I am just past my sixtieth year. Wisdom gained? It's hard to say. Looking back at my teenage and college years, I can see that I've let go of some of my youthful grandiosity and sense of entitlement—the demon-sprite that told me I'd certainly win the Nobel Prize in science, a second one in literature, and maybe cure cancer along the way. Sometimes I miss that demon, though, and I wonder if the "realistic" expectations of my later years are really a kind of surrender—settling into old age, rather than raging against its limitations.

In my sixth decade, intimations of mortality are never far from me, and I can now read Robert Frost's deeply-felt poem, "Nothing Gold Can Stay," with an understanding I never had in my college literature course:

Nature's first green is gold
Her hardest hue to hold.
Her early leaf's a flower;
But only so an hour.
Then leaf subsides to leaf.
So Eden sank to grief,
So dawn goes down to day.
Nothing gold can stay.

I was raised in the Jewish faith, but, like many American Jews, I have found much wisdom in the Buddhist tradition. In his book, *Everything Arises, Everything Falls Away*, the Thai meditation master Ajahn Chah teaches us "…to look in the present and see the impermanence of body and mind." He speaks of the peace that comes from "letting go" of attachment—whether to the newest electronic gadget, a rigidly-held belief, or even a beloved friend or family member. When he was five, Ajahn Chah's father died suddenly, and this left a deep wound in the young boy—one that prompted him to meditate on the fragility and transience of human life. I lost my father to cancer when I was 17, and the loss surely shaped my sense of the world as a place where nothing could be taken for granted.

In my teens and twenties, I saw mortality as something to defeat—there's that cure for cancer again—but lately I have to come to see death in somewhat more conciliatory terms.

No, I don't welcome the idea of personal oblivion. But having imbibed the teachings of the Buddhists, and their Greco-Roman cousins, the Stoics, I now try to see death as one of the necessary processes of Nature. The late Steve Jobs reflected a bit of this Stoic wisdom in his 2005 Stanford commencement speech. "No one wants to die," Jobs said. "Even people who want to go to heaven don't want to die to get there. And yet death is the destination we all share. No one has ever escaped it. And that is as it should be, because Death is very likely the single best invention of Life. It is Life's change agent."

Now, I don't want to convey the mistaken impression that I spend all day contemplating the prospect of death! My life is packed with the blessings of a wonderful marriage, a challenging career and—more recently—the indolent pleasures of semi-retirement. In fact, I've been thinking a great deal lately about *gratitude*, and how fundamental it is to what the ancient Greeks called *eudaimonia*–"the flourishing life." First, of course, is gratitude for life. How many people in the history of the world have lived beyond 60 years? (In 1900, life expectancy at birth in the U.S. was about 50 years – now it is over 77). In the Jewish faith, we are instructed to begin each day with a prayer of thankfulness, known as the *modeh ani*. In English, the prayer goes, "Thankful am I before you, living and eternal King, that you have returned my soul within me with compassion; abundant is Your faithfulness." The Rabbis tell us that *we return God's faithfulness with our own* by expressing a prayer of thanksgiving each day.

I have to admit, I don't say the exact words of this prayer, but each day, I do find a way of thanking God for life and health—and for the innumerable blessings in my life. When I think of the woes I have witnessed over the last 30 years—the sorrows and sickness of friends and loved ones, the suffering of so many of my patients—I would count myself a fool if I didn't feel immense gratitude for my life. I am especially fond of a Buddhist teaching, which I have taped to my computer monitor: "Let us rise up and be thankful, for if we didn't learn a lot today, at least we learned a little; and if we didn't learn a little, at least we didn't get sick; and if we got sick, at least we didn't die; so let us all be thankful."

And, with the advancing years, I have lost patience with a certain type of intellectual virtuosity. As a college student, and even as young physician, I devoted a good deal of time to esoteric subjects in philosophy and theology—I can still spout off St. Anselm's "ontological argument" proving the existence of God! In my later years, I have become much more interested in personal ethics—not so much the theory, as the everyday practice. In my book, *Becoming a Mensch*, I tried to develop the idea that each of us can become a better person by practicing a few simple habits in our daily lives—for example, civility, honesty, and kindness. I am guided by a wonderful teaching from Rabbi Abraham Joshua Heschel, who said, "When I was young I admired clever people. Now that I am old, I admire kind people." Indeed, kindness is arguably the core value within all the major faiths. When the Dalai Lama was asked to explain his religion, he replied, "My religion is very simple. My religion is kindness." Imagine what the world would be like if each of us were to put that teaching into practice! I fall short of the mark every day, but I find that my life is greatly enriched by the mere effort of practicing kindness.

And yet, and yet: I come full circle to the epigram that begins this essay, from the late Stanley Kunitz's poem, "King of the River." (Kunitz died in 2006, at the age of 101). Ostensibly a poem about salmon, "King of the River" is of course much more than that. When he was in his 70s, Kunitz was interviewed by Chris Busa, for the *Paris Review*. Kunitz said of this poem, "It may be pertinent that I experienced a curious elation while confronting the unpleasant reality of being mortal, the inexorable process of my own decay. Perhaps I had managed to "distance" my fate—the salmon was doing my dying for me."

But the lines from "King of the River" that have always stuck with me are these: The great clock of your life/is slowing down,/and the small clocks run wild." What did Kunitz mean by this? I don't know, and maybe Kunitz didn't either. (In his interview, he made the point that, "A poem has secrets that the poet knows nothing of. It takes on a life and a will of its own.") Yes—and a poem holds meanings for its readers that often go well beyond the intention of the poem's author. I understand the "great clock" of my life as simply my own limited, "biological" time as a human being. But what of "the small clocks" that "run wild"? For me, these are the myriad plans, hopes, desires, projects and passions that I may never realize, but which are an unkillable part of my nature and being. They are the beneficent remains of that demon-sprite that inhabited and drove me in my youth. And while I honor the emotional "equanimity" the Stoics called *ataraxia*, I find it a bit too staid and stolid for my later years. I pray that the small clocks of my life run wild for whatever time I have been granted.

Ronald Pies MD is a psychiatrist affiliated with Upstate Medical University and Tufts University. He is the author of several books on philosophy and spirituality, including *Everything Has Two Handles, Becoming a Mensch*, and *The Three-Petalled Rose*. His novel, *The Director of Minor Tragedies*, is forthcoming.

"Nothing is inherently and invincibly young except spirit. And spirit can enter a human being perhaps better in the quiet of old age and dwell there more undisturbed than in the turmoil of adventure."

George Santayana

ASPECT OF AGING

Maureen Flannery

I stare into droop-lidded blue eyes
identifying kindness in your skin's slow slackening
that lets me see my own chronology, as gentle,
if imprecise, as garbled first words of our grandson.

We can be each other's mirror
in the faithfulness of honest aging,
not to recoil from smile lines
creased into our present presentation
as the folds of an old love note.

My own growing old is put at ease
by the truthful loosening of your face
with dark places where the sun has shone
ambiguous rays upon youthful days of field work
and vigorous outdoor play.

Secure in each other's gaze
we learn to claim the countenance we've earned
like a paycheck for a job well done.

Watching your face become more handsome,
framed in gray, I think we may go graciously
to that place of knowing
past all recall of pertinent matters
toward a final way of being
where nothing matters but love.

Maureen Tolman Flannery's most recent volume of poems is *Tunnel into Morning*. Her other books include *Destiny Whispers to the Beloved*, *A Fine Line* and *Ancestors in the Landscape*. She is a wood-carver, toy-maker, and home funeral guide. Her poems have appeared in fifty anthologies and two hundred literary reviews.

ENOUGH SPACE TO SEE MYSELF

Jim Van Buskirk

I have been turning 60 for the past six months. Actually, of course, it's been happening for much longer than that, but I've only really noticed it recently. It started so gradually, and it crept into my life so insidiously I didn't realize it was happening.

I struggled with how to mark this momentous occasion. A big party, a series of smaller celebrations, an exotic trip? Dinner with my boyfriend, Allen? A night of theatre? I couldn't motivate myself to make a decision. In the end I invited a handful of friends for dinner at my house. My longtime caterer friend prepared and served a deliciously simple repast of eggplant parmigiana, sliced summer tomatoes, garlic bread and fruit crisp. I provided the ice cream. It was a wonderful evening, one of many intimate gatherings orchestrated over several weeks.

In the past months I have been reprioritizing, slowing down. Once known as *au courant*, a culture vulture, a man about town with his finger on the pulse of art, theatre and literary offerings, I am now hopelessly, haplessly, happily out-of-touch. At first I thought I had become jaded, was perhaps depressed, but now I am coming to appreciate my state as positive. I see it as a positive response. Nothing gives me more pleasure than sitting in my Adirondack chair in the backyard reading a book and watching the hummingbirds dart into the gurgling fountain. No longer much interested in traveling, certainly not by plane, but rather staying close to home is an unanticipated pleasure. I feel as if I am preparing, as someone aptly put it, for the adventure of "the third half of my life."

I'm shifting, becoming someone other than the person I've always assumed myself to be. With no clear sense of where I'm heading, as if I'm traipsing across a bridge of wood and rope suspended from one side of a steep ravine to – I'm not at all sure where the other end is attached, or even if it is.

During my life I have moved from "Diddy" to "Jimmy" to "James" to "Jim;" from questioning kid to out and proud gay; from former Unitarian to secular Jew; from full-time librarian to part-time book group coordinator to free-lance writer, researcher and archivist. The appellation "semi-retired" applies to more than my work life. Those shifts in identity are not what I'm talking about. It is rather a divesting of extraneous roles, a de-cluttering to see who I might have been all along.

When I began conscientiously my campaign to discard, I was amazed at the detritus that had accumulated in my apartment. I use the passive voice because I couldn't possibly be responsible for all this, or could I? I began slowly, first looking around in closets, cupboards, and then the basement to see what I had long ago stopped seeing. Friends expressed surprise, telling me that my flat never appeared cluttered and expressed wonder at how I could be disposing of so much stuff.

Every morning for weeks I woke with a new goal. Before I even rose from bed I thought of a new object to assess or area to attack. There was the bicycle I hadn't ridden in many years despite my repeated intentions to dust it off, re-inflate the tires, and roll down the hill. I decided to give it to someone who would really enjoy it, and not feel guilty about *not* riding it. And the clothes – perfectly good – but knew I'd never wear again, they went into bags until long-crammed drawers were completely empty. Space I'd never imagined could exist began to manifest. Even those shopping bags of pink and blue tile, harvested years ago for an imagined mosaic project, now I acknowledged would never materialize. So satisfying to dump them into the trash can to be carted away.

A big bin of cards and letters I had been lugging around for decades. I scanned each birthday card, postcard, letter from various friends, family, and lovers remembering the person who wrote it – but only vaguely the person to whom it had been addressed. He seemed to be simultaneously present, forgotten, and deceased as were the eclectic collection of correspondents. Notebooks of journaling, half-finished poems, drafts of essays all went into the recycling bin. Pangs of wonderment went with them. Why had I saved these? What did they represent, and why was it now, suddenly, so easy to discard them? It seemed I was not so much discarding the note cards, the pieces of paper but, perhaps even more so, the person who had until now been hanging onto them.

Books were shelved two deep on three tall bookcases. I bravely started a pile of titles I might be able to part with. With each volume pulled out and held in my hand I started a new pile. I will never read this again. I can always get a copy from the library. I don't even remember where this one came from, much less why I've kept it. Piles were placed into bags, then repacked into boxes. If I can part with this, then I don't need that, I reasoned. This process began to be fun. I returned borrowed books to friends and overdue books to the library. Another casting off to see what I truly valued.

One morning, lolling in bed, I looked across the room to my collection of records. I hopped up and immediately began sliding the albums out, each one telling a story of the time I bought it, listened to it obsessively, then moved on to another disc. Every Joni Mitchell album – up to *The Hissing of Summer Lawns* – the French chanters, original Broadway cast albums, motion picture soundtracks – including the first two LPs I ever bought: *Flower Drum Song* and *The Music Man*. Here they are, fifty years later: still much loved, well-worn but seldom played. I have been carting around these vinyl disks in their paper sleeves and cardboard covers for decades... winnowed a little after the advent of cassettes and CDs, but mostly kept merely because I have always kept them. Classical, jazz, rock, they each reflect the music that buoyed me during depressions, allowed me to wallow after breakups, and distracted me through periods of boredom. From first thing in the morning until I fell asleep at night, they were the soundtracks to my life. And now I didn't need them anymore. Sorting through them, suddenly I became aware that I am no longer the person who had appreciated them, memorized the sequence of every track, every pop, hiss, and skip. Into bags and boxes I tenderly placed them, saying a sweet, sad farewell to my former, faithful friends.

Until, that is, I came across one album entitled *Pamela Brooks*, copyright 1982. Pam, a local chanteuse singing a standard repertoire, had recorded four songs written by a former lover of mine. I had moved to San Francisco in the early 1970s, unsure of myself, inexperienced in my sexuality, and ill prepared for a relationship. A brilliant pianist and composer, Bob introduced me to a world that revered Stephen Sondheim, Barbara Cook and Bobby Short. He proudly introduced me to his friends – all artists, actors and singers. Suddenly I was in a sophisticated milieu of cocktails, dinner parties, and backstage gossip. In time, we moved in together. This was my first domestic partnership.

Ours was never *not* a charged relationship. Bob, I later learned, was childish, needy and drank too much. After drunken fights and morning after promises, I finally found the wherewithal to leave him. After we broke up, he called my father to tell him I was gay, threw a carton of eggs at my front door in the middle of the night, and threatened to slash my car tires.

Now, holding the album in my hand, I remember he told me he had written those songs for me. Since I'd never had a love song written for me, this must have been real love. But when later I learned he'd told his other lovers the same story, I couldn't help but chuckle. When I heard he'd died of AIDS in New York in 1996, I wept at the loss of such a great but troubled talent. Instead of discarding the album, I replaced it on the shelf. I wonder why there are some things I am not quite ready to part with.

Against the wall of newly weeded bookshelves is a cabinet on top of which are arranged various family tchotchkes. I assess this altar of sorts. On the wall above hangs a pastel portrait of my brother and me, dated 1960. It was sketched on the afternoon of the evening I played my accordion with the Lawrence Welk Orchestra at Pacific Ocean Park. In its blond wood frame it once held pride of place in my mother's bedroom and now hangs here close to mine. Below is a small dish filled with my brother's and my combined baby teeth, so scrupulously saved by my mother our "tooth fairy." I can't yet bring myself to dispose of them.

I pick up the red lacquer nested dolls that Mom brought back from Russia, and which I interpret – whether she did or not – as a memento of her long-hidden Russian-Jewish roots. These I put in the discard box. What about her bronzed baby shoes on the rectangle of marble engraved "Anne-Marie"? No, not yet. Nor the ceramic figures which adorned my parents' wedding cake, saved through decades of a discordant marriage, only to end ultimately in divorce.

For years her wedding dress hung in the family's garage. Then I happened to notice, in its place, hung only a ghostly, aging translucent bag. When did she finally bring herself to throw it away? I still find unfathomable Mom's late-in-life claim that, despite it all, the highlight of her life was her marriage to my dad.

Mom's high school ring, her lapel pins. My grandmother's ring – which Mom finally gave me after over two decades of estrangement – a gold filigreed *coupe de champagne*, the only one remaining from a set that had belonged to my beloved great aunt. I dust off all these objects and rearrange them back on the altar.

The one remaining object is a large, black, metal tea canister imprinted "Mariage Frères," which only I know contains some of Mom's ashes. They have been there for almost five years now ever since I'd taken them with the idea of scattering them in the Seine on my next trip to Paris. The idea of returning her ashes to the place of her birth seemed appropriate at the time, but I have no foreseeable plans to be in Paris and suddenly I'm ready to release them. I contact my friend Margaret, now permanently living in Paris, about her next visit to the west coast. Margaret had met Mom on her last trip to the City of Light and now said she'd be honored to help me with this final act. But complications ensued – as they will in life and in death – and Margaret and I didn't connect this spring as planned. She suggested mailing them but research quickly revealed that FedEx, DHL and UPS don't accept human cremains. Using the US Postal Service would be a hassle for Margaret so I will wait for her visit next year. The decision made, I feel lighter. I dust the canister and replace it on the altar.

The more I sort, the easier it becomes. My boyfriend, a committed collector – in his terminology and a packrat in mine – offers to help. He is surprisingly adept at assessing what should be kept and what tossed. I return many of the thoughtful, generous gifts he has given me over the years. I don't want to hurt his feelings, but I have long maintained and told him before that "I don't want objects," and still the Audrey Hepburn mugs, the pansy plates and the Jiminy Cricket pins are proffered. Finally, he seems to understand and, ruefully, he takes back some of the objects. I start a box of items to give to friends, prepare piles to donate to the Salvation Army, to the Friends of the Library, to recycle or to throw away. Then I take notice of the things I plan to keep and suddenly, I can start to see more clearly. I still have a long way to go, but slowly I am creating enough space to begin to see myself.

Sixty feels "old". Turning forty, fifty, and fifty-five were no big deal. But this one seems big. As if I have reached the pinnacle and from here it's all downhill. No more expectations of myself. No more need to please. It's liberating, but in a bittersweet way.

I ran into a dear friend yesterday and we found ourselves discussing at what age to apply for Social Security benefits. After a few minutes I told her I was thinking even further down the road, that Allen and I had recently purchased a niche in the San Francisco Columbarium. She seemed nonplussed. When I announced that I had just asked a potter friend to create an urn for my ashes, she blanched. I felt good about preparing for the inevitable, but then realized perhaps it's not an appropriate topic for casual conversation.

I have begun to read books about living well and dying well. I am relishing every moment, whether it is a mid-afternoon nap, lunch with a friend, or revisiting favorite movies. As each day ebbs, and time passes, I reflect *not* on whether I have any regrets, because that seems rather useless. And I am less invested in planning for the future. Instead, I focus on the present, on being here now, as the expression has it.

The clutter, it's cleared away. The detritus of my life, cleared out. I am ready, finally, to become myself.

Jim Van Buskirk has co-authored two books and co-edited two nonfiction anthologies. His essays and articles have been featured in various books, newspapers, magazines, radio broadcasts, and websites. A popular public speaker, his most recent project is a yet-to-be published family memoir entitled *My Granmother's Suitcase*. www.jimvanbustkirk.com

ONE TREASURE I KNOW

Vidya Vonne

In my 20s and 30s I was always looking forward: to the next relationship, the next career move, the next town, the next vacation, even the next yoga retreat. But, as I enter my 60's – like so many of us – I feel compelled to look back: how did I get here? What people or activities lasted and which fell away? Is there anything, anything at all that I did that is worth passing on, that someone younger might see and feel, "I should definitely emulate that!"?

Of all the people and all the activities and adventures, one thing stands out for its lifelong benefits: Yoga. I began the physical practices – the postures, breathing and vegetarian diet – at the age of eighteen. For some years I lived in a Yoga institute in Los Angeles and later at a Yoga Ashram in Connecticut. For those years the practice was more intense, in later decades out in the world I did only a "maintenance dose," some years not even that. But, I always returned to it, I never forgot, and now at the age of 60 I have not missed more than a day a week in many years. Some days I teach yoga, even teach others to teach, some days it's just my personal practice in front of my altar.

But, it is my life's companion and the results are here to be felt and seen every day of my life.

Since the term "Yoga" is used these days to mean a million things, I should be specific as to what I mean by it. The philosophy behind Hatha Yoga, or the physical yoga, is a portal into Spirit via the body. Yes, it cleanses the system when combined with vegetarian Yogic diet, and yes, the body gets more flexible and strong, but along with that, the mind and one's energy gets turned inward and gently focused – through the body – to a space that some call being "centered," a place where the mind ceases to be tossed here and there by what's going on outside, but is focused from within, even throughout the day when the senses are turned outward. The way I see it is, it is not physical exercise that I'm referring to here, although the body is used – it is a mental or energetic or spiritual practice done through physical means – with wonderful lifelong physical side benefits. It has been a surprise to me that my body has been such an unexpected beneficiary.

I could have just read about Yoga and spirituality. I could have focused on meditation. I could have just learned to pray. I could have become a philosopher or a pundit, a tantrika or a shaman. But, somehow I chose Hatha Yoga as my main spiritual practice, and the side benefits have blown me away. My body is light, flexible, fit and a lovely place to live in. When others, even those much more spiritually advanced than me, complain of the "inevitable" aches and pains of getting old, of their back aches, high blood pressure, chronic injuries, allergies, and arthritis, I marvel that I feel like a teenager! My weight is the same as it was in high school, I can walk forever and dance every night. I sit easily on the floor, can sleep on any surface. I can think of no other explanation than my lifelong Hatha Yoga practice.

Looking back, I think of everything else: the travels to exotic places, the college degrees, the relationships, the spiritual quest. And, the tragedies were there too: the deaths, the losses, the heartbreaks. But, what in the end has endured? That I felt good while all the rest happened. That my body is a pleasure to live in. That I'm happy in my skin. This is surely not the most important thing in the world. But perhaps it's my small contribution – my small offering to the world in the form of the life I've led. For me, it has been important to take care of my body. I believe if I take care of my body, it will take care of me. I've never had much money, but the saying "Health is Wealth," makes sense to me; I'd rather feel good than be rich, and I count my riches with every breath, every step, every day.

Rev. Vidya has been practicing Integral Yoga Hatha for 40 years. She began teaching at 18 and now trains teachers at Satchidananda Ashram/Yogaville. In 2008 she deepened her dedication to the spiritual teachings behind the physical yoga by becoming a Minister of Integral Yoga. She holds an MFA in Creative Writing and has served as a Massage Practitioner for the past thirty years.

"The great thing about getting older is that you don't lose the ages you've been."
                                    Madeline L'Engle

FINAL ADVENTURE

Doris Thome

When Stephanie leads me upstairs to see my patient for the first time, she says, "You'll see how David keeps us all on an even keel."

Stephanie knows little about her husband's rare disease since so few cases have been documented and there is no time frame and little data available. Aware only of the changes that are happening to David, she hopes he still has several years remaining.

Stephanie leads me toward the staircase cluttered with packed boxes. The couple have moved here from an elite Los Angeles suburb where both had been college professors.

"David wanted us out of the L.A. area and surprised me with this condo. It's exactly what we talked about getting some day: ocean views, large vistas and plenty of sunlight but I never dreamed how challenging it would be to move from a large house to a condo one third the size of our former house."

As we climb, I think how unsuitable this is for a person who is wheelchair bound. He needs an elevator.

David is ensconced in a king-sized bed in an upstairs room. He watches us, his face open and inviting. He leans against pillows and a heavily padded headboard. Beyond him, one entire wall of the room is windowed with ocean views. David's aquamarine eyes, as blue-green as the Caribbean Sea, are surrounded by long, dark eyelashes above suntanned cheeks. He is observing me while I take in his surroundings. David is one of those individuals who gives you one-hundred percent of his attention. Despite the room's captivating views, I become riveted on my patient.

"This is my husband, David. David, this is Jessie."

Upon being introduced, the large dark-haired man slaps his hand down onto the comforter, "Jessie. My mother's name was Jessica," he exclaims obviously pleased, and flashing a broad grin. "She was the most incredible woman I have ever known. I know I am going to like you."

Left alone, the two of us spend time getting acquainted, the enjoyment of our exchange obvious to both of us. I notice immediately that his speech and diction are that of an accomplished thespian. It is a joy to listen to him. I can see him in a classroom setting throwing out his net of animated lore and hauling in his fascinated students.

As we review his status, David, in his erudite way, responds to the questions before they are asked; he knows the drill. His upbeat manner and precise answers withhold nothing. I like this; he makes my work easier. In no time my paper work is fleshed in. I understand what his wife Stephanie was saying. It is true, David is very alive. Despite the rare disease that ravages his body, his mind clicks with excited curiosity.

It is time now to check on the physical part of my visit: vital signs, air exchange, grip, reflexes. Non ambulatory patients usually have circulatory problems and where bone is covered by skin without the padding of muscles, the skin takes a beating. I check David's spine, elbows, heels, shoulder blades, buttocks, and coccyx. He promises me he will ask his wife to locate his heel protectors. In an attempt to restore circulation to the reddened areas and lower extremities, I later notice that David's thoughts have drifted elsewhere.

Finished with the body scan I excuse myself and move into the dressing room where his medical supplies are stored. One of my tasks for this newly assigned hospice patient is to give him his daily injection of an experimental drug. Reading the data that accompanies the medicine I learn this particular medication is highly toxic. It can leak out and cause serious skin irritation. This means the skin and tissue must be pulled to the side as the needle is inserted. This procedure is called Z-track. After injection, when skin and tissue are released, both will return to cover up the site and prevent leakage.

I don gloves to protect my own skin, before drawing up normal saline to inject into the vial to dilute the powdered pharmaceutical. I then shake the contents in preparation for the daily injection. When thoroughly dissolved, I draw up the required dose of potent drug, dislodge all bubbles, and, syringe in hand, I return to the bedside.

Pensive, David looks out at the view, then he turns to face me. I sense his smile is forced. I wonder why. Something has changed. The fake smile fades quickly and it is obvious that David has something to say but isn't quite ready. Deep in concentration, he closes his eyes, lifts his head and takes several deep breaths. Nodding to himself, David's face relaxes back to that calm but sure-of-himself person I met when I first entered his room. He lifts his hand off the blanket, not far…

just enough for me to see his upturned palm. Head turned my way, he pauses as I read his universal signal to stop. Syringe and alcohol wipe in hand, I wait to hear what is on David's mind.

His gorgeous aqua eyes bore into my blue ones. "Jessie," David begins, "I have made up my mind. I have decided to stop the injections."

I feel unsure of what to say to him, I'm verbally shut down and feel helpless. This is not something I considered.

"Do you realize what this means?" I stammer. Of course he knows what it means. David, more that anyone, knows. I push on. "… how quickly you can deteriorate if you stop?"

David is not only a strong communicator, he reads people well. As he watches me, I see he has no hint of confusion about his decision.

"Yes, I do understand the ramifications. For five, almost six-years I have struggled. I've been in a wheelchair for three of those years and retired from teaching even longer. I knew I would eventually get to this point. It was your name. Jessie. I cannot explain it further, but the time feels right; I am ready to join my mother."

After a few seconds I realize I am holding my breath. I feel apprehension, yet am fascinated at the same time. This patient has no qualm; the more he talks about being ready the more comfortable he seems. But not me. Everything about this case is different. Usually I am the one teaching and leading others toward acceptance that life is waning. Now I am being led.

David has motioned for me to sit on the bed. As he talks to me with deep sincerity, I listen to his adventurous life, travels, family and how blessed he feels. He points toward the bank of windows before him. "When I sit here – that tree, that lone eucalyptus – that is where I shall be every morning. It's Stephanie's plan for us to commune each day upon her waking. I gave her a hard time about this, told her she's never been on time in her life, that it would be a darned hard, skinny perch for me to wait for her to wake up. She just smiled that beguiling grin of hers. She knows we're destined to be together – the only way left to us.

"You know," David continues dreamily, detached and talking to himself more than to me, "there is one thing I have not done and I am getting darned excited about it." I let David go at his own pace.

His eyes shimmer and his exhilaration becomes contagious. David announces with great aplomb. "My final adventure still awaits me. I have not died."

I observe him closely. David's face glows with happiness at what he envisions. Can a person be both vibrant and serene, because this is what I see. He's excited. He accepts death and he is graciously dusting off its welcome mat. I sense I am in the presence of a man who is already on another plane. David's clarity makes me realize how flawed are my own narrow views.

Shaking my head, I realize what David must have gone through with those who believe the only way to live life is to push through no matter what. Anything less is considered suicide and for many, if not most, this stamps a person as depressed or insane. There are those who fall into this category for one reason or another, but many do not. In my opinion, the medical field is myopic in so many ways and this is one of them.

David turns to study my face. "You understand, Jessie."

This is not a question. Somehow David knows I comprehend what he is seeing and feeling. Not yet grasping how I could have moved from being anxious to being comfortable with my patient's decision, suddenly I too feel at peace.

Then I know my work is finished. I pack up and dispose of the experimental drug. I lean down and, without words or regret and with mutual acceptance, our eyes say our silent goodbyes. Strangers only an hour ago, we are now far more than friends. Transcended, we are now deeply connected.

I'd seen David once in my life, and the man has managed to change how I view dying. If only I could teach this. Most Americans are uncomfortable around death; they don't want to discuss or think about it. I've viewed many deaths and the only ones that were the least uncomfortable were those who feared it. According to David, dying is just another adventure. I smile every time I recall his words.

This is Doris Thome's first submission for publication. She spent her final career years, ten of them, as a hospice nurse. Her first attempts at writing were non fictional stories, but she finds fiction beckoning. She is presently polishing her hospice manuscript, currently titled, *The Journey*.

CRASH TO CRASH: A LONGER VIEW

Julian Langley

1929

Almost a third of the way through the twentieth century on the afternoon of September 4, 1929, the streetcar slows and before it stops, Sarah leaps to the street. She clutches her purse tight to her chest, and she rushes through the crowd. She fights back tears. Without pausing, she runs the blocks directly home to her working class row house there in Cleveland, Ohio, where one of the nation's greatest steel producing centers stretches along the dirty, smoke-smudged shores of Lake Erie. She's sweaty, feels faint. She bites her lip to keep from whimpering.

"I've lost it. All of it. Every penny I worked so hard for. Gone," and she collapses in the chair at the kitchen table. She runs her hands across the red-checkered oil table cloth, clenching and re-clenching her fists. "The bank froze everything!" She catches her mother Hilda's expression out of the corner of her eye. She reads in her mother's face sheer terror. *Black Tuesday,* the day will come to be known. A day neither Sarah, nor her mother, Hilda, nor the nation was soon to forget . . . the final, devastating, most disastrous stock market crash of that year – and of that era.

"They're saying what's happening to us won't stop here. It's happening in cities throughout this country. It's going to spread out into farms and ranches and to every industrial nation across the globe." Sarah's voice is barely audible.

Sarah is my mother. Hilda, my grandmother, and harder working German-English immigrants, you'd never see. Their story is a part of my story. Their dreams, not unlike my own.

1950s

"Look here," my mother Sarah says to me, now a teenager, as she opens the thick file of impressive looking documents while we sit on the couch side by side. "See how I ranked at the top of my high school class. And take a look at this, my early acceptance to university to start the teacher training program. You have to understand that being a secretary, a nurse, or a teacher were the only occupations open to women back then in the '30s – and look, this Certificate awarded to me for my work in the Cleveland-based Dow Chemical labs even before my high school graduation. I'd go there every afternoon directly from class. My bank account was growing even before I reached fifteen.

"But, could I go on into science? I mean professionally? Not likely. Investigative science wasn't open to me – even with all the credentials I'd earned. Nursing would be about it, but my science interests focused on research. That's where my fascination lay, but what could I do? So instead, I shifted my sights to what was available. And in my case, that was teaching – an equally noble profession, I chose to think."

I watched as Mother Sarah lifted her gaze. It was as though she were seeing across the decades. Then she went on, "That was back when we looked on banks as safe-keepers of our hard earned money, and before the FDIC was put into place to protect us from the losses so many of us endured." For ten oppressive years our personal lives, as well as the nation and the world, would know hardships unlike any they'd experienced that century.

What I had come to know about my mother, and her mother before her was that they had grit. Their dreams had teeth – and feet, and astounding adaptability.

Back to 1941

"Come along. This is important for all of us," Dad calls to my mom and Grandma Hilda, and the rest of the family to come together in our little Ohio house. We gather close in, pulling chairs over from the dining room table.

Mom and Gram untie their aprons. They lean in close while Dad adjusts the knobs on our little, Delco table-top radio. Then we hear something. Dad adjusts the sound still further and we catch the thin, New England, socially up-scale accent and we know it's the voice of President Franklin Delano Roosevelt, "Yesterday, December 7, 1941," he is saying, "a date which will live in infamy – the United States of America was suddenly and deliberately attacked by naval and air forces of the Empire of Japan . . ."

Numb. Mute. Each of us senses immediately, in our own way, the gravity of these words. We'd heard about the massive military buildup starting in 1940. Just as Roosevelt was vying for a third term at the presidency, 16,300,000 of America's young men from across the nation registered for the services – the largest peace-time military draft in the history of this nation, then or any time. If life hadn't been hard enough already, what did it have in store for us going forward?

Would Dad be drafted? He's still young enough and besides during his university days he'd been in the army reserves. And how about my big brother, David? He's just turned seventeen. My body suddenly goes cold.

President Roosevelt is talking about wartime austerities, rationing, everyone putting their shoulder to the cause, and I am paralyzed.

Sometimes, when I could snatch even a few moments from the tasks so much a part of living on a large Ohio acreage where Mom and Dad and Grandmother Hilda had moved from metropolitan Cleveland – all of us depressed and worried, and war weary – I would saunter off, our dog, King, along beside me, to the newly mowed alfalfa hay field stretching out to the east of our home. If I went at just the right time on one of those hot July evenings there'd be the fragrance of clover, mingled with the clean scent of sun-drying hay. If I lingered just long enough, fireflies would come out, flickering and darting from blossom to blossom. They had a way of bringing a playful and much needed whimsical touch to those precious moments that became my childhood dream time. They freed me from the anxieties of life pressing in around me. And there, I'd find a sheltered place, lie back and recount the stories that brought me right alongside the events my folks had lived before we gave up so much of our lives during those years. Our ears were always close to the radio. New names had come to people our days: Winston Churchill, Clement Attlee, and Stalin, Khrushchev, Mussolini, and most fearful of all – Emperor Hirohito . . . and . . . Hitler.

Then later: Hiroshima. Nagasaki, and later still the Berlin wall, and their aftermaths . . . lest, as the philosopher George Santayana coined the aphorism, "Those who do not read (and heed) history are doomed to repeat it" . . . and did he overlook something?

Along with saved foil gum wrappers, buying Savings stamps, and the war reports, never discarding a single rubber band, there were the whispers. Strange, secret goings on never spoken of openly: internment camps, concentration and extermination camps. Who, and what, and where? And our imaginations ran wild. Only later, well after the Armistice was declared in 1945 did the news spread its way across into the middle states, shocking and stunning us with accounts of unthinkable human atrocities.

Yet, we also lived our own day-to-day cautions during the war. "I'll be stopping by the Volkert farm after school today," Mother says to me, "so we'll get home a little later than usual." Mother, by this time, is a respected educator in our area – always going out of her way to find ways to be of help to her young students, and this time, their parents too. "Jonus has missed too many classes lately. I need to see what I can do."

Mrs. Volkert, heavily built, her blond hair a braid encircling her head, her cheeks flaming. lips full, stands before us at the open door. She greets us, there on her Ohio farm, her German accent, thick. Then, with no pretense, no leading up to it, she nearly collapses into my mother's arms. That's when I learn, standing there by my mother's side and looking up at them both, why Mrs. Volkert is so emotional, and why her son has so many absences from school.

"They've taken Albert." Mrs. Volkert weeps openly. 'And we hear by short wave radio, they've taken him to fight in the U.S. naval air force. Do you know what that means? He'll be fighting exactly opposite to my brother, Hans, flying for the Luftwaffe. I'm sorry Jonus has missed school, but who is there to run the farm and keep the cows milked and the butter and cheese made? I'm all alone." And in that moment, I come face to face with what I come to know as my first experience with war's ironies and I sense a strange feeling – one I later identify as compassion tormented - for both ally and enemy alike.

In time, we rivaled President Roosevelt's ingenuity with our own works programs. Dad, along with a neighbor boy, dug our well there in the Ohio countryside. Sent a water sample off to his university Alma Mater for testing. We'd learned how to plant, then save and dry seeds for the next year's yield. We'd learned how to raise and deal with livestock, birth more for the next season while putting away meat for the coming year. We canned. We dried. And with the advent of freezing, we rapidly shifted from dripping ice blocks to refrigerators.

"I, for one," I'd teasingly boast, "I am the direct beneficiary of President Roosevelt's New Deal." Along with his initiation of WPA and the CCC in the mid-1930s, he saved not only the nation's countless unemployed artisans and labors, but something else too. He contributed, as a direct byproduct, to people, even kids like me . . . and right on into this very millennium with the resourcefully and powerfully built structures that serve us on into our times: dams, parks, all marvels of human engineering and workmanship.

We scraped, we saved, we created and made do out of what others might regard as worthless. "Nothing," we are cautioned, "nothing is to be thrown away, not if there can be seen the slightest usability remaining to it."

Like the day mother says to me, "Listen closely, Dear," and I give her my attention but I'm also aware that the early Spring morning is awash with sun and the fragrance of lilacs. Lavender blooms turn the moist, morning air pungent and sweet. "First, feel the fabrics. Now remember, use more than just your eyes. If they're not entirely clean, yet the material is in good condition, keep in mind we can always launder them and hang them in the sun to sterilize. And, don't worry about a hole here or there. Tears we can mend. What we can't do is reconstruct the fabric quality. So, study everything. Keep an eye out for the largest, most re-useable pieces once we cut the garment apart. I know you'll do a good job."

I wonder to myself if mother knows she's talking to me as though I'm older than my eleven years. But then, it feels good to think she can rely on me.

Then Mom says: "It's like playing with puzzle pieces." I'll learn to spread out the odd shaped fabric pieces on the dining room table. She teaches me pattern making, fitting, smocking, pleating, gusseting and the magic of a whole, newly constructed garment, fashioned with verve on her Singer sewing machine and later worn with grace. Even a touch of pride.

Mainly what I learn is we just do what must be done. What I come to see is that need, together with resourcefulness can propel toward high satisfaction. "It's like finding fun within work, "Mom says to me, "and all with a thankful heart, that is."

When I say a thankful heart, that's because of what Dad had his own way of saying to us. "Here's the order of priorities," Dad would lay them out to my brother and me. "Whenever contemplating any activity – think: God first, then others, and yourself last." And that came to be our family mantra no matter how tough and pinched life became.

But Dad wasn't done there with his admonitions. Where he was concerned, I came to understand, was that the Ten Commandments were not enough. It's the eleventh that capped them all.

"Listen up, "Dad would say and when my brother and I put down what we were doing and turned to him, he'd remind us of what Jesus said in the Book of John where he's talking about the importance of the virtues of peace and goodness and patience and joy and meekness and temperance . . . "but the most important of all," it says and Dad emphasized, "is love."

And sure enough if those words didn't stick with me through all these years. Served well, too, and stood the test of time. They held their place all through the 50s and the burst of affluence following the war that ended in 1945. They offered a counter-balance to the 60s when our nation's youth rebellion took center stage all way around the globe. They offered a groundedness through the 70s when the national mantra seemed to shift to "I, me, my, mine," and on through the tsunami of the self-esteem movement when the way folks seemed to see life was, "Anything I want, I get." "Me, first. Others, after me. And God? Well, who the heck is that?"

Such were the principles Mom and Dad taught me that soon expanded far beyond mismatched fabric pieces and saving pennies in a Mason jar. They come into play when I am faced with numbers of contrasting, conflicting things, ideas, and even people . . . forces that appear at first glance to be blatant opposites, desperate, jarringly incongruent, yet with the Rumpelstiltskin-like demand that in the face of impossibility, possibility is to be found – that there too is to be found the precious gold of workable relationships, of peace from chaos, and of beauty within its opposite.

2000s

So here we are in a whole new millennium, sitting in the midst of an economy that began its recent, shocking crumble in 2007, and growing toward full repair at a dismally slow pace. And, how does this particular crash, again felt world-wide, and resulting in what is now called the *Great Recession,* differ from its cousin, the *Great Depression?* We're being told – or, more accurately *reminded* – that just because we can qualify to borrow money doesn't mean we should – either individually or as a nation. That the stock market and the national lottery have not-so-subtle characteristics in common. That loss is a fact of life. That greed is problematic. That true humility is characterized by amazing strength, not weakness. That being self-absorbed is just that. That forgiveness and second chances have incredible power, meted out with discrimination. That to prepare and be frugal still makes sense, as does that bit about honesty being a pretty good policy. And as for that 11th Commandment, the one that marks love as the highest human virtue, well yeah, seems like that's still a work in progress, as is gentle, every-day human kindness. And yet where hope and optimism are concerned, they sure stand the test of time and turmoil, as does the still-to-be-plumbed-extent-of-power of a thankful heart. So, what about those family mantras now? Old fashioned? Out of date? Time to toss them aside?

Hmmm, well, just as I'm not ready to put the family heirlooms out on E-bay, so I think I'll not be tossing out those nuggets any time soon. I see these precepts, first passed along by Grandmother Hilda, and adapted to the times by Mom Sarah, and filed for ready reference by me, as far too precious to dump or trample, or allow to spin off into either the landfill or void of cyberspace. Perhaps like the games we used to play with bits and pieces of what other folks might call worthless stuff, I choose not to degrade them, nor the memories they evoke, nor the creativity they inspire, but rather to preserve them, revere them, and to revel in the wonder of it all.

Retired educator, historian and freelance writer.

LET THE CLOCK RUN WILD

Kenneth K. Cohen

As I look into the mirror
Closer, closer, nearer, nearer
What I see with each fine line
Where past and future intertwine
Is all that waxes also wanes
So little of my youth remains
Except within my inner child
Uncompromised unreconciled
To anything but being free
Of feckless age as destiny.
No, I say, it's not the end
My butterfly waits round the bend
To claim my spirit and to soar
My here and now forever more.
Uncompromised, unreconciled
It's time to let the clock run wild!

Kenneth Cohen is a published children's book author: *Imagine That! A Child's Guide to Yoga* and *Songs of the Sandman*. Kenneth lives in Santa Barbara and owns an Espresso catering company.

Appendix

Companion resources in the genre of published works for, by, and about golden agers in American culture.

AARP, *The Power of Experience: Great Writers over 50 on the Quest for a Lifetime of Meaning*. New York: Sterling Publishing Co., Inc., 2007.

Alford, Henry. *How to Live: A Search for Wisdom from Old People While They Are Still on This Earth*. New York: Hachette Book Group, 2009.

Davidson, Sara. *Leap: What Will We Do with the Rest of Our Lives?* New York: Random House, 2007.

Erickson, Erik H. *The Life Cycle Completed*. New York: WW Norton & Company, 1994.

Erickson, Erik H. and Joan M. Erickson, Helen Q. Kivnick. *Vital Involvement in Old Age: The Experience of Old Age in Our Time*. New York: WW Norton & Company, 1986.

Fonda, Jane. *Prime Time*. New York: Random House, 2011.

Fowler, Jan. *Hot Chocolate for Seniors*. Bloomington, IN: Balboa Press, 2011.

Hawkins, M.D., Ph.D. David R. *Power vs Force: The Hidden Determinants of Human Behavior*. Carlsbad, California: Hay House, 2002.

MacLaine, Shirley. *Sage-ing while Age-ing.* New York: Atria Books, Div. Simon & Schuster, Inc., 2007.

Munsey, Brenda, Ed. *Moral Development, Moral Education, and Kohlberg* (Lawrence). Birmingham, Alabama: Religious Education Press, 1980.

Morgan, Robert F., with Jane Wilson. *Growing Younger: How to Measure and Change Your Body's Age.* Concord, California: Amazing Experience Press, 2004.

Pillemer, Karl, Ph.D., *Thirty Lessons for Living.* New York: Hudson Street Press, Div. of Penquin Group, 2011.

Schachter-Shalomi, Zalman, and Ronald S. Miller. *From Age-ing to Sage-ing: A Profound New Vision of Growing Older.* New York: Warner Books, 1995.

Thomas, William H., M.D. *What Are Old People For: How Elders Will Save the World.* Acton, Massachusetts: VanderWyk & Bunham, 2004.

Tornstam, Lars. *Gerotranscendence: A Developmental theory of Positive Aging.* New York: Springer Publishing Company, 2005.

Vaillant, George E., M.D. *Aging Well.* New York: Little, Brown and Company, 2002.

Wykle, May L., Peter J. Whitehouse and Diana L. Moris, Editors. *Successful Aging Through the Life Span: Intergenerational Issues in Health.* New York: Springer Publishing Company, 2005.

About the Editors

Judy Warner Scher

A writer, editor and publisher of non-fiction books for more than twenty years, Ms. Scher is recognized for excellence in books focusing on philosophy, religion and biographical material. Amongst other publications, she compiled and edited three anthologies: *Transformation of the Heart*, *The Dharmic Challenge* and *Inspired Medicine* as well as having published numerous stories and essays in books and small publications. *Let Someone Hold You*, a memoir edited by Ms. Scher, won the Christopher award in 1997. Ms. Scher was editor and co-publisher at Leela Press. She honed her editing skills working with Eleanor Friede, best known for bringing the novella *Jonathan Livingston Seagull* to publication.

Judy Warner Scher's career in writing and publishing followed many years in the theater as an actress, singer, composer/lyricist and producer, a career she revisited recently as she created, wrote and produced shows for local TV called *Dare Kids to Dance*. A woman of many talents, Ms. Scher was a mediator for the state of Virginia and worked in Hospice first as a Pastoral Care Assistant and later as a Bereavement Coordinator.

Dr. Jewell Reinhart Coburn

An award-winning author of books for adults and young readers, Dr. Coburn traveled widely studying the history and culture of the world's peoples. She authored books used in the nation's schools and universities designed to foster inter-cultural appreciation and understanding. She received multiple awards for her Series, "The Search for Shared Values." Each of the forty carefully researched stories from varying ethnic traditions are found in: *Beyond the East Wind: Legends and Folktales of Vietnam; Khmers, Tigers, and Talismans: From the History and Legends of Mysterious Cambodia; Encircled Kingdom: Legends and Folktales of Laos* plus *Enchanted Necklace,* revealing a little known fact from Hmong history.

Dr. Coburn's Cinderella Series is based on her research of the origin of the fairy tale theme, first appearing in China and traced through SE Asia and on to France, contributes richly to the body of work in this genre.

Also by Dr. Coburn: *Authentic Voices: Women of Insight Talk about Real Life Challenges;* and *From Inkling to Opus: Unlocking the Stories within You.*

Dr. Coburn was instrumental in founding the first Hospice in the Conejo Valley of Westlake Village, Thousand Oaks, and Newbury Park, California, and published *Death and Living,* a practical guide with spiritual emphasis for interfacing with terminal patients, their family members, and concerned others. Additional information: www.jewellreinhartcoburnbooks.com

www.ingramcontent.com/pod-product-compliance
Lightning Source LLC
Chambersburg PA
CBHW022353040426
42450CB00005B/164